KEEPING MY DISTANCE

Pip and Me on Castle Hill

KEEPING MY DISTANCE

Susan Bulmer

The Pomagne Press

First published in Great Britain 2004 by
The Pomagne Press
P.O. Box 122
Ripon
North Yorkshire
HG4 3ZX

ISBN 0-9548537-0-9

Some of these chapters were previously published in
the form of articles in *The Times, The Sunday Times*, and
Harpers & Queen magazine.

This book is printed on acid free paper.

Typeset by Rowland Phototypesetting Ltd
Printed and bound in Great Britain by
St. Edmundsbury Press,
both of Bury St Edmunds, Suffolk

CONTENTS

POEMS

ACKNOWLEDGEMENTS

Carla Carlisle is Renaissance woman, brim-full of talent. She is also a close friend to whom I owe a large debt of gratitude for having given me inspiration, encouragement and the benefit of brilliant editing. Without her vision and support my writing would have remained in the bottom drawer of my desk.

My thanks go also to David Elsy. His impressive skill with computers, including my beautiful silver and white Apple iMac, has been greatly to my advantage.

For J.E.B.
14.6.87

Having found you again
I want to ring you round with growth marks
Like those on the severed trunk of a tree
Where my marbled whorls of plenty
And callouses of grief,
The detail and the distance
Are there for you to see.

INTRODUCTION

My Grandmother used to wake each morning anxious that she could not remember what it was that she was worrying about. This book is not so much a collection of worry beads but of memory beads which I have examined and polished over time. Some of them remain opaque and others I hold up in search of the translucence of understanding. I have changed a few names and places, but I hope that, where there is truth, it is able to speak for itself. Necklace or noose, these beads are irrevocably linked to my past.

When I lived in Washington D.C. in the early sixties, I read a newly published book, *Advise and Consent*, by the American writer, Allen Drury. It was described as 'a tale of intrigue in high places where men are pitted against each other over momentous matters of state, unleashing passions of love, ambition and revenge'. I have always been fascinated by politics and in the paradoxes and dilemmas of daily life. However, my writing is not politically correct. I resent this modern discipline which has been foisted upon us all. Frederick Forsyth considers political correctness to be a form of fascism. It is certainly a kind of tyranny, but not a new one. In 1932, when my father went up to Trinity College, Oxford, he found himself confronted with a choice that all Freshmen were expected to sign up to. Pinned on the noticeboard were two columns headed *Fascists* and *Communists*. He spent a sleepless night considering which he thought he might be. He could not sign under 'Fascist', but did not go to Spain to fight. Some of his friends did and one or two never returned.

My mother believed that publishing my writing was showing off. When I rang her in Dorset to say I had a piece in *The Times* she said, 'You know we only take *The Telegraph*, so bring it down when you come next weekend.' Parents are life's great levellers.

When I was a child I wrote to my parents in Burma and the letters are intact, kept safely in two large shoe boxes. Why did she keep them? I am fairly certain she never re-read them, so clean and untouched are they. Perhaps they reminded her of a kind of bereavement, which left its mark, both on her and on me. Before she went back by boat to the Far East to join my father, she addressed a great many cream envelopes so that

I could write to her there. I was six years old and performed as scribe for my four-year-old brother who was not keen on writing.

Charlie, my eldest son, asks if retribution is the reason for writing about my past. Is it a settling of scores? It is true that I was too immature to handle some of the situations I found myself in, that I met with unexpected hostility and that at times I felt misunderstood. I do not think it is self-indulgent to try to make sense of your life by writing about it. Indeed, self-indulgence is not trying to make sense of your life. I shine a light into the dark places, not only in my life, but also into other people's lives. I have tried to double-knot the memory beads when I trespass in these rough areas.

Memory is a fallback; it can only be true to the one who remembers. Can it really be lost or is it not just damaged, broken into boulders, splinters, fragments and shards of reflected light, like a collapsed building? We are all built upon the sum of our memories, tilted mirrors of what we perceive to be there, from the inside, looking out.

I have never been able to understand the concept of infinity. I have seen the curvature of the earth, flying twice the speed of sound at Mach 2 on Concorde. I have walked in the Malaysian rainforest, seen the Australian outback and the Russian Steppes, been soaked by spray from Brazil's Iguazu Falls and slept on a Persian rug under the stars in the Rub al Khali, but it is the finite horizon of memory that distils my vision.

The profound happiness and the security I yearned for came relatively late in life, with my second marriage. In 1987 we met again, after a decade, in the lobby of the House of Commons. The lofty Pugin arches swirled above our heads as he approached me carrying a black, furled umbrella. Over dinner in that riot of Gothic high drama my happy ending began. I have been able to explore the dark canyons of memory from a plateau of light and love.

Susan Bulmer
Studley Royal

BEGINNING IN BURMA

The day I was born the sirens screamed in Maymyo, in Chauk, Mandalay, Rangoon, Moulmein and Meiktila. A dreadful daytime jackal wail which set the pi-dogs howling. In compounds and dirt streets, bare brown feet ran around in panic and confusion, bundles on heads, babies in arms. It was rumoured that the Japanese had come over the border from Thailand and, mounted on elephants, they were massing along the banks of the wide Sittang river to the south, intent upon crossing in order to take Burma's capital city and stronghold of the British, Rangoon.

In the small British Military Hospital in the hill station of Maymyo I breathed my first breath at about 8.00 p.m. on the 23rd December 1941. I was brought into the world by a Scottish doctor, a missionary in China who had fled the invading Japanese to make his way overland into Burma. The hospital was clean and tidy and outside its whitewashed walls were covered in Bougainvillea and

1

Canna carefully spaced in circular beds on the lawn of broad spiky grass.

Maymyo was the summer playground of the British and a constant social round focused on Government House, the club, polo, tennis and the golf course. The small town (reminding them of Chertsey or Sunningdale) was five thousand feet high built on a large and fertile plateau in the Shan hills of Upper Burma. Mandalay was to the south. The surrounding area was mostly dense jungle with rivers cutting through in deep gorges with spectacular waterfalls, their sources being in the mountains of China a hundred miles away. For as long as anyone could remember the local hill tribes had been at war. It was said that 'the land of Burma is blood red'.

In January 1942 the Japanese invaded from Thailand and captured Moulmein and then Rangoon. They very soon had supremacy in the air and on the ground.

My young mother, recovering from childbirth and cholera, was forced to flee from the approaching enemy with me, her newborn baby, taking with her a young Karen woman called Chit-Su. For luggage she had packed in great haste a single kitbag containing her jewel box, nappies and tins of Ostermilk. She buried the family silver in the garden and everything else – wedding presents brought out from England, my father's Purdey guns, photographs, rugs, silver and furniture – she was forced to leave behind in Maymyo. After a harrowing time of worry and uncertainty and a dramatic life-saving gesture from a train driver who gave her water from the tank of his engine for my bottle, with Chit-Su, she managed to get on one of the last flights out of the jungle, seated on the floor of a Dakota transport aeroplane which flew out of Shwebo to Chittagong in East Bengal. She then found herself in a refugee camp on the banks of the Ganges near Calcutta. Somehow she managed to contact her uncle, A.J.S. White, who was influential in the Indian Civil Service and he quickly got her out and away into the hills. After the war my mother tried unsuccessfully to get in touch with the charming, intelligent Karen girl without whose care and help she and I might not have survived.

Meanwhile, my father, 27 years old and a Major in the 10th Battalion, Burma Rifles, found himself behind the lines with virtually no food, medical supplies or ammunition. He and his company of men began a journey of six months retreating from the Japanese and walking three hundred miles across mountain ranges and deep jungle valleys. One of his tasks was to see that his peacetime employers, The Burma Oil Company's refineries in Chauk, Syriam and Mandalay among others were destroyed so that they would be of no use to the enemy.

There were times when the flesh of monkeys and snakes was all that there was to eat, and drinking

Daddy, Chit-Su with Pip, me and Mummy in Dalhousie, India in 1944 at his Christening

brackish leech-infested water did little to slake a constant thirst and often brought on dysentery. He was guided and helped throughout this time by the knowledge and skill of his batman, Gopal, a member of the Naga hill tribe.

An episode too terrible to remember: vultures were spotted wheeling overhead and the loud buzzing of a million flies was heard close by. They had come upon the hospital train out of Mandalay which had been ambushed and left stranded in the blazing heat, abandoned by its terrified Burmese crew who had run off into the jungle leaving over a hundred people dead and dying. The order was given to end their agony.

My father's memory of Burma during these years was painful, because he felt again the suppurating blisters on his feet and the deprivation and horror of the long trek through suffocating jungle and torrid plain. He survived the ordeal, reaching Naini-Tal in the Northern Province of India and turned up having grown a surprising red beard which helped dispel rumours surrounding the paternity of his red-headed baby daughter. My brother was born in Dalhousie in 1944. The family moved to Quetta where my father attended the Staff College and was promoted to Lt. Colonel. He was eventually posted back to Burma and found himself in Rangoon for V.J. Day.

Many close friends had lost their lives in that terrible war and having to fight an enemy who revered and even welcomed death was disturbing. My father's health was damaged by the traumas he had suffered but we did not realise this until some years later when he had a stroke while only in his forties. Mercifully he largely recovered.

GRACE AND FAVOURITE
DAYS WITH GRANNY

Bramley was a Victorian rectory built of stone with little architectural merit, surrounded by a large garden, stable yard, tennis court and a paddock or two at the foot of Castle Hill. My grandmother moved there from the grander Castle House at the other end of the small Wiltshire town of Mere early in her widowhood.

At the outbreak of war, during the period known as the 'phoney war' when nothing much seemed to be happening, my mother answered the front door bell at Castle House to find a soldier in uniform having dismounted from a motorcycle. He presented himself to her with a salute and an explanation that he was the cook. My mother said 'There must be some mistake. We already have a cook.' This was the first the family knew that their house had been requisitioned by the army for occupation by British troops. So Granny piled boxes and hastily packed trunks into the attic and she and her two daughters moved first to The Chantry and then to Gaspar Cottage in Stourton. Her son, Philip, only 21 years old, was in the Welsh Guards and was posted overseas. When Granny was allowed to return four years later she found the house in a bad state with damage to the floors and wood panelling and thefts of several items, including valuable stamps from my grandfather's albums, stored in the attics. Two hundred pounds was given as compensation for the army's occupation.

Under the pointed eaves at Bramley were a series of low-ceilinged rooms, one with a trunk of dressing up clothes kept for charades and the Mere Carnival. I found a silver dress with net petticoats and a Red Riding Hood cloak with a satin lining. It had been arranged that my small brother, Pip, should join me in the carnival procession through the main street to the sports ground dressed as a pixie wearing my green bloomers with pipe cleaners stuck in his hair. However, he refused to take part and made one of his 'dreadful scenes' as Granny called them.

Miss Winterbottom lived at the top of the house. She was the cook but Granny said she was also a 'Distressed Gentlewoman'. This sounded tragic to me. I thought she was clearly a have-not in terms of belongings, but she did not lack imagination and I often sought her company. Looking like the stone obelisk towering above the gardens at Stourhead, Miss Winterbottom opened the door to me at the top of the attic stairs,

'I am melting wax,' she said, 'I am making bridge

Granny opening a Fête

pencils and dipping the ends in different colours and when it sets I shall wrap them up to give away at Christmas. Tomorrow you can help me make snowmen egg cosies out of felt with black hats and scarlet mufflers.'

I gazed out of the window at the 14th century church where my parents had been married on June 1st 1940, the day of the evacuation of Dunkirk. In the distance I could see the Saxon hilltop town of Shaftesbury in Dorset.

'Pam says she hopes never to have a daughter because she so much prefers little boys,' I told her with resentment.

My Aunt Pam had been Crossed in Love and was always referred to by Granny as Poor-Pam who explained that the prefix was attached in early childhood when, after a quarrel, my mother had tipped her goldfish down the lavatory and pulled the plug. As I passed Pam's room on my way down to the hall I could hear her wind-up His Master's Voice gramophone playing 'Run Rabbit Run'. She also had a record of 'Who Stole My Heart Away' and 'You Are My Lucky Star'.

I passed the Cold Bathroom with its dark green linoleum on the floor, which curled up at the joins. The bath stood on lion's paw feet and on the door was a notice which read:

'The lease of this well watered spot is short,
Extension can't be got,
Haste then, for in ten minutes more
The next will thunder at the door!'

I found this mystifying because I never could imagine
who would thunder at the door since we were a house-
ful of women except for my six-year-old brother,
Pip, and Frank, the gardener. I had only ever seen him
come upstairs once and that was when I found Pip
stuck halfway down with his head wedged through the
banister. I tried to get it out but, to shouts of pain and
fury from my brother, I ran down to find Granny.
She was doing flowers in the scullery, secateurs in one
hand with a trug full of stalks and leaves on the wooden
draining board.

'Pip is stuck, Granny,' I said.

'Stuck? Stuck where, Darling?'

'On the stairs with his head through the banisters.'

She put down the secateurs, went swiftly to the back
door and screamed 'FRANK!' Granny always screamed
at Frank, believing him to be stone deaf like her sister,
Aunt Dora. Pip and I used to test him by whispering
and he would hear our every word. Before the war Frank
had been the groom but now that there were no horses
he was the gardener. With a saw in hand he mounted
the stairs in his bulbous well-worn leather boots where

10

swords and revolvers and pictures of dead and dying men in the mud of the trenches lined the walls. The turned oak post of the staircase had to be sawn in half to release Pip's head.

Granny drove her grey Standard car with confidence. Chairman of the Magistrate's Bench and a governor of the Prison and School, she dressed in sensible shoes and a tweed skirt and a hat discreetly adorned with the Welsh Guards leek brooch. Her bedroom looked over the lawn sloping down to gloomy shrubberies. The bed seemed very high with its carved walnut headboard. Her Bible was much read and to hand, as was a tin filled with Digestive biscuits. There were photographs of my dead Grandfather and Uncle Philip and framed documents in which they were Mentioned in Despatches. An air of great loss surrounded Granny but she was always serene although her smile was sad.

Pip and I had a Dutch governess called Miss Lever. Known as 'Mee-Lee' she was much liked. She did not make us eat up our leftovers by serving them up meal after meal as had her predecessor, Nannie Taylor, and she warmed our Chilprufe vests and pants on the fender in front of the nursery fire in cold weather before we put them on. There was friction in the air when Miss Lever's authority was undermined by Granny:

'Oh Jean, do let the darlings have it!' she would say when either of us was about to be denied something.

Aunt Dora usually came to Sunday lunch. She had been born deaf because her mother had contracted German measles during her pregnancy, but she was clever at lip reading. As a child she had been taught to speak by the new method which had been successfully used with the American deaf and blind child, Helen Keller. My great-grandmother had taken Dora up to London on the train from Gillingham every week for treatment. Aunt Dora was an eccentric dresser and was fond of bright orange and purple, usually wearing both colours at the same time. Granny found the effect unnerving. She would mouth every syllable in a slow, deliberate way when speaking to her sister and then, only slightly turning her head sideways, would say to the rest of us at her normal speed:

'Why is it that Dora has such dreadful colour sense?' Aunt Dora's sharp eyes never missed such an aside and she always understood her sister, however quickly she moved her lips.

A broad grey spaniel called Jane lived at Bramley. Granny did not care for animals and she belonged to Poor-Pam. Jane constantly wanted to go out, and when out, wanted to come in again. This seemed to happen most often in the drawing room where French windows opened into the garden. Pip decided it would be sensible if he were to make a permanent hole in the glass for her convenience and so he simply kicked in the bottom pane.

Bramley

'Pip has broken the drawing room window, Granny,'
I was quick to point out.

'I haven't broken anything,' Pip assured her. 'I have
made something – a special hole for Jane!'

Granny followed us back into the drawing room and
seated herself in front of the piano on the seat which was
full of music books. She played 'Weel may the keel row'
and Agnes swept up the broken glass and summoned
Frank.

The morning room was our favourite place where
there was a bum warmer (club fender) around the fire-
place. After lunch we would turn on the wireless at a
quarter-to-two for Listen With Mother which we called
Listen Without Mother since ours was six thousand

13

miles away in Burma, and I danced to the music at the beginning and end.

Granny told us about her grandfather who lived at Norton Hall near Bath and hunted his own pack of hounds. He was a music lover and when he felt a creative urge coming on, he used to summon his family from their beds at any hour of the night to take up their instruments and play in the family orchestra. Granny's mother, Minnie Beauchamp, played the harp, looking angelic in her cambric nightgown.

Granny's niece, Gwen Beauchamp, wrote later in her journal of those years at the turn of the century:

'My earliest memory was when I was three and a half years old. My sister, Cynthia, who was three years younger, was very ill. I was standing on the landing of the Grange in Midsomer Norton when Dr Waugh, our family doctor and Evelyn Waugh's grandfather, came out of the night nursery with my mother and said, 'As you know, your baby has meningitis and I am very sorry, Mrs Beauchamp, there is nothing more we can do for her and I am afraid she will not pull through.' Actually, she did recover and lived until she was nearly seventy and died of arthritis. She lived a full life, was married and had a son, was good at all games and played tennis for her county. In 1902 we moved from The Grange to Norton Hall when my grandfather died. It was a large house and

*Pam, Granny, Miss Lever, Pip and me
(Granny wrote on the back of this photograph:
'Why is Susie looking so woebegone?')*

estate with a staff of eight indoor servants from butler
and footman downwards plus a nursery governess and a
governess who came out from Bath daily to teach us until
we went to Roedean at the age of fourteen. There was a
large home farm which my father farmed very well,
although his chief interest was in the local collieries, of
which he owned two with a share in others. Most of his
tenants were either his farm and estate workers or
miners. We had large stables and Dad was Master of the
Wells Harriers. Robin Athill writes in his book *Mendip,*

'perhaps the most famous local Master was Louis Beauchamp of Norton Hall (1902-1913) where up to two hundred would sit down to breakfast before the opening meet.' He also owned some racehorses and won the Great Metropolitan in 1908 with Father Blind, which was stabled at Norton Hall when retired.

I used to ride every day, but soon after leaving school I started getting very stiff and was in a lot of pain. My father made me have a hot soda bath every day but the pain became steadily worse and after a week I had to be lifted on and off my horse. The doctor diagnosed acute rheumatism and said I must never ride astride again. I was not keen to ride side-saddle and so I have not ridden since.'

Louis Beauchamp was my great grandmother's brother. He is buried in the graveyard at Midsomer Norton where his grave is marked by an imposing tombstone. His brother, Frank, was knighted for services to the coal industry.

Granny's only son, Philip Franey Matthews, was killed in the war aged only twenty-one. He died in the desert at Medjez el Bab in Tunisia in December 1942. I imagine that when my parents left us with Granny they hoped we would act as balm on the wounds of her bereavement. We were much indulged at Bramley and we loved her deeply. There were no suitable schools in

Burma in those days and the climate was considered dangerous for small European children. My father and his sister had also been left behind by their parents and went to boarding schools in Scotland from a very early age when Grandfather Murray was employed by Octavius Steel in India.

I read a great deal: *The Secret Garden*, the *Pollyanna* books, *Little Women* (I loved Jo), *Little Lord Fauntleroy*, *The Railway Children* and *The Children of the New Forest*. I was frightened of *Strewelpeter* and could hardly bring myself to turn over the page on which I knew there was a coloured picture of Suck-a-Thumb and the demon man with huge scissors who was about to cut off his thumb.

The scissors also reminded me of a story I overheard my Aunt Joan telling Granny. One of her maids at Charnage left suddenly, and, on turning out the attic bedroom after her departure, a dead baby was discovered in a drawer with scissors piercing its heart.

We sometimes went to tea with Mrs Bailward at Stourton. The garden of her house ran down to the lake where we swam, fished and rowed the boat in and out of the boathouse. Mrs Bailward had only one foot, the other having been amputated when she got gangrene after stepping on a rusty nail when getting out of bed in Malaya. She taught me to play Mah Jong on a hand-painted ivory set.

Castle House

My hobbyhorse lived in a loosebox in the stable yard. He was made of a lisle stocking stuffed with rags, and had button eyes and a felt nose which Miss Winterbottom had helped me make. The bridle consisted of a headband, throat lash and nose band of brown dressing-gown cord, and two brass curtain rings for the snaffle bit, and long reins which I clutched when astride the broomstick which was thrust into the head. My hobbyhorse was hunted, hacked, mucked out and fed with loving care.

The loose boxes at Bramley were empty of real horses. It was at The Kendalls where my great uncle, Blandford

Matthews, lived that I made friends with Eric the head groom. I liked to help him clean the shiny black cobbled floors, heap more gold straw on to already knee deep beds, refill the salt licks and water pails and climb into the hayloft to stuff hay nets and mix bran mashes, not forgetting the bottle of beer (Matthews' Ale) which went into Idlewild's evening feed. Idlewild had won the Prince of Wales cup at Larkhill and been petted by the Queen. Over the manger in each loose box was a board with maroon lettering on it with the horse's name: Aladdin, Seagull, Neddin's Lady and Idlewild. Fantail pigeons with pink feet flew in and out. Their dovecote was in a gable on the roof of the stable block with a weathercock on top. Two large stone mounting blocks stood outside. The tack room smelled of linseed oil, Brasso and leather and was festooned with stirrups, bridles and bits. On the racks were saddles, girths and collars, and harness for the trap. In her youth Aunt Ina had hunted side-saddle to hounds which I found hard to imagine.

At Castle House, before my grandfather died, Granny had managed to avoid having anything to do with horses until a grey pony and trap appeared as a surprise birthday present. Her confidence grew in time and she began to enjoy her daily jaunts along the lanes. Sadly, it all came to an end. Plodding sleepily along in the fullness of a summer afternoon, the air scented with honeysuckle and meadowsweet, and only the tip of her whip visible over her head over the high hedgerows, she distractedly hooked the reins she was holding over her head. Minutes later the pony, aptly named Speedwell, started when a man and a dog appeared suddenly in a gateway and she bolted. Granny was unable to extract the reins from around her neck and when the light trap overturned on a bend in the lane she was thrown out and dragged for some considerable time.

My grandfather, Arthur Matthews, returned from three years in the trenches during the First World War, seemingly physically intact, although he was to die when only forty-two years old from peritonitis caused by inadequate army surgery for the removal of his appendix. However, the mental traumas of that time had left their mark. My mother remembers a secret macabre game he used to like to play with her when he would lie prostrate behind the sofa like a dead body and she had to run round and round pretending to be a rat, biting his legs from time to time.

In summer the Shetland pony, Timmy, was put into the back of a mill lorry and taken down to Studland where the family took a house. The children rode him bareback into the sea until he was swimming.

Deaf Aunt Dora hunted on a cob with a docked tail. She often felt sorry for the fox and her hunting days came to an end after an episode which was witnessed by an outraged Mrs Troyte-Bullock who told the Master.

Aunt Dora was lagging behind the rest of the Field when she saw that the fox was doubling back, heading for a ramshackle hen house. She reined in her cob, dismounted and slammed the door, trapping the animal inside. Hounds were soon upon her, speaking on the scent, but they disappeared in confusion, baffled by the closed door and Aunt Dora's defiant stance in front of it.

When I was twelve I was presented with the fox's brush at the end of a day's hunting and bloodied by Cobbie, the Huntsman-in-Chief of the South & West Wilts hunt. I was told not to wash my face for twenty-four hours. I took care not to look in the mirror. Much of my time out hunting was spent trying to remain in control of my pony, Firelight. I also made sure I was nowhere near the kill because I felt so upset. Firelight was certainly not the 'dear little fellow' my mother thought he was. He had a very hard mouth and should have been ridden in a pelham bit rather than a snaffle. Cousin June told me some years later that she had always suspected him to have been a rig – a botched castration job and that would have explained some of my difficulties.

My mother and her brother and sister were made to hunt twice a week during the season by their father. My mother's pony, Splinters, would take hold of the bit when excited and became unstoppable so his rider inevitably fell off. Since she had six or so uncles among

My mother on Timmy
with boy groom

the Field, one or other of these hearty gentlemen would remark disapprovingly that her breeches were very dirty. She became so nervous that after the Meet she would manage to lose the others, daub spots of mud on her face and on Splinters, and after a suitable interval would return home. There she would tell of the good run they had had, and even where they had killed.

Granny used to tell me that she had seventy-six first and second cousins. Some of their offspring got together for Uncle Geoffrey's summer birthday. All the children had numbers strapped onto them like jockeys and a cross-country course was followed through the bluebell wood, over a field and back up through the garden. A collecting ring with stakes and ropes marked the winner's enclosure at the finish. All the jumps, obstacles and the water jump were expertly made.

Uncle Geoffrey was known by us to be 'difficult'. He had a very red face and kept to his study which was lined with silver cups, some enormous, and mostly won by his racehorse Streak, a point-to-pointer so famous that the Prince of Wales asked to see him when he flew down in his light aircraft to meet his Duchy tenants. Streak's story is an interesting one. A trainer of racehorses owned by the Royal family was asked to scour the country for an outstanding steeplechaser for the Prince of Wales. After many months a fine horse was found in Ireland and with much excitement he was shipped over to England. On the voyage across the Irish Sea the boat ran into a severe storm and the horse lost his balance and was thrown violently onto his knees. On arrival the animal was in such poor shape that it was decided not to show him to the Prince and, feeling that his racing days could now never happen, he was put into a bloodstock sale in the Cotswolds. Uncle Geoffrey heard about this and, having inspected the damaged legs, he realised that with the right treatment, all was not lost. So he bought Streak and took him home to the rolling acres of his Wiltshire farm where he soon regained his health and, in time, was to become an outstanding steeplechaser.

At the time of the Prince's visit in July 1923, just under half of the many thousands of acres farmed by the Whites was Duchy land. When the Prince came down Streak was turned out on Keysley Down and with difficulty was caught and cleaned up for the Royal visitor. At the end of lunch in the Matthews' Ship Hotel in Mere, the Prince was told that Streak was ready to be inspected. HRH looked at his watch and said that he had to get back to Windsor as it was getting late.

At Bramley tramps sometimes came up the drive to the back door where Agnes would give them a mug of tea and bread and dripping. Agnes and Mrs Foot were Granny's maids and they had been born and lived for some years in the workhouse in Mere. This vast ugly building filled me with fear when we took the laundry there to be done. It surprised me that Agnes and Mrs Foot could be so sweet and gentle. Castle House where Granny used to live had been turned into a Borstal and its 'Bad Boys' came to play cricket on the lawn with Frank and my brother and me.

Mr Stone the saddler had a shop not far from the bottom of the drive. He sat working in the window wearing rimless spectacles and a black leather apron. His shop smelled of linseed oil, sweat and horse.

Mr Stone died aged a hundred and Mrs Stone pulled down the blinds until she joined him eight years later.

When Granny drove her Standard car through Mere she sometimes drew up outside Waltons in the main street and hooted her horn twice whereupon a white-coated Cyril Foot would run out and take down her order. Waltons was a miniature Harrods in Wiltshire where one could buy furniture, groceries, Pringle twinsets and even coffins, which was enterprising for a shop in so small a town.

BINDWEED

The time came when school was considered necessary for Pip and me. Granny decided upon the boys' prep school at Zeals which was two miles away and newly situated in an Elizabethan mansion which had for generations belonged to the Chaffyngrove family. I was one of eight girls among ninety boys. The grounds were extensive and beautiful and included a dank and gloomy lake. One day we were told never to go near it again and I later learnt a peat-preserved body of a young woman had been discovered there. It is known that a grey lady haunts the house together with the persistent tapping of a walking stick on the stairs whenever a member of the old family is nearing death. The nursery and servants' quarters still smell of sweaty plimsolls and school-cooked cabbage.

An ambitious school play was produced that year – *A Midsummer Night's Dream*, and I was chosen to play Titania and had eight foolscap pages to learn:

'. . . Come sit thee down upon this flowery bed While I thy amiable cheeks do coy And stick musk roses in thy sleek smooth head And kiss thy fair large ears, my gentle joy.'

Pip was Mustard Seed and his best friend, Bill Taylor, was Moth. Pip had only two words to learn. Standing in a line with Pease Blossom, Cobweb and Moth he had to say after Bill, '. . . And I.' But he forgot and there was a long silence and the prompter had to intervene from the wings.

That Christmas as we sat on the bum warmer in the morning room at Bramley eating hundreds and thousands in sandwiches and toasting crumpets in the fire, Granny said, 'Darlings, Father Christmas has sent a special message to you both. He said he has so many presents for you that you must be sure to put out a pillowcase each at the end of your beds instead of a stocking.'

On Christmas Day we went to The Kendalls for dinner where sixteen members of the Matthews family gathered together for the meal which began early because the staff were allowed to go off duty by 10.00 p.m. I wore a long velvet dress and Pip his Murray of Atholl tartan kilt with silk ruffled shirt, sporran and buckled shoes. Great Aunt Ina's Christmas tree was as tall as the ceiling and lit by real candles. Soda syphons were ready in case of fire. Granny told me we must never draw attention to our cousins Nony and June's hair as it was false. My eyes were therefore riveted upon their hairline for much of the evening. As children, they had caught ringworm on their scalps after playing apple-in-the-bucket with some village children at a fete in the garden at The Kendalls. The bucket was full of water and the children had to bite the apple and bring it out clenched between their teeth with hands tied behind their backs. Nony and June had to have their heads shaved and daubed with iodine and Aunt Ina took them to London every week for two months to have the newly discovered radium treatment on their heads which was thought to hasten new growth. As a result their beautiful red hair never did grow again and they were completely bald except for a few surprising brown wisps which escaped from behind their ears under identical clumsy red wigs. Sadly, Nony was to die of a brain tumour in middle age.

After hot punch, watered down for us, we went into the dining room where the long table was decorated with lengths of cotton wool on which were a nativity scene, Father Christmases and sleighs, reindeer, robin red-breasts, snowmen, angels, holly, crackers and numerous lit candles. Nanny drifted about, the Christmas spirit having flushed her out of the attic flat where she had been 'put out to grass' for fifteen years. She looked incredibly old, was dressed entirely in white and long grey hairs grew on her chin.

I gazed around at the oil paintings on the panelled walls: black-eyed ancestors, a highland scene with monarch of the glen, a turbulent shipwreck and an exquisite still life of flowers, a beetle and a butterfly among grapes, with a teardrop beneath. This last picture was said to have been left to my mother in Uncle Blandford's will and I gave it my special attention. It was a Dutch masterpiece by Rachel Ruysch painted in the early 17th century. (It subsequently disappeared.)

Pip was no longer sitting in his place but was crawling about somewhere under the table. There was a squawk from June – Pip had burnt her leg with his sparkler and ruined her silk stockings which were the last she could get from her ration book. Uncle Blandford rose to toast The King, followed by Absent Friends which included our parents and Poor-Pam. Then we all went into the drawing room to play games. First of all, items laid out on a tray had to be memorised in three minutes and then written down when the tray was removed. The second game was to feel objects sewn up in muslin bags by Nanny and to identify them. Aunt Ina was relieved to discover the grape scissors which had vanished the previous week. Consequences was played next: Who met whom and where and what they said followed by what the consequence was and, lastly, what the world said. We then played charades and I was given ALMIGHTY to do which I acted out after whispered consultation with Granny as ALL-MY-TEA. The party ended with Come-And -Sit-On-My-Lap which I disliked because the hisses always grew louder when I approached my favourite grown-up, Cousin Sheila, and died away when I drew close to one of the boring aunts, turning to claps when I sat in the chosen lap.

Cousin Sheila was Home From Abroad, but she was still in disgrace because she had deserted from the WRENS during the war. Had she returned to England before Peace was declared she might have been imprisoned. Crossing on a ferry from Dunoon to Greenock she took off her uniform in the lavatory and stuffed it out of the tiny porthole into the sea. She then dressed in her mufti which she had brought in a knapsack and simply disappeared, eventually to meet up with her boyfriend in South Africa. When Uncle Blandford heard of his daughter's extraordinary behaviour he hastily despatched a telegram which read: DO NOT LET YOUR KING, COUNTRY AND FAMILY DOWN STOP RETURN TO SHIP IMMEDIATELY STOP DADDY.

Granny loved Uncle Blandford, but it was a Dangerous Liaison because he was her late husband's brother. I called him That-Man-Again for obvious reasons. Small and slight, with sharp features and a quick wit, he seemed alive and alert in the way small animals are. He had inherited a considerable fortune with the brewery and nearly two hundred pubs but he bicycled to his office at Wyke in Gillingham each morning. There were two identical Wolseley cars in the garage – identical so that nobody would realise that the family owned more than one car.

Uncle Blandford told me that as a character-building exercise he considered it necessary to know what it was to be poor and that he, as a very young man, had been sent out to Ceylon by his father where he found himself with so little money that he was forced to live on a diet of dry dog biscuits. I was slow to understand that this was a joke and that there were at that time only a very few mangy curs and jackals on the island who had certainly never seen a biscuit of any sort.

As a Major in the First World War Uncle Blandford had a distinguished record serving in Gallipoli and then in Palestine. He won the Military Cross besides being Mentioned in Despatches. With the outbreak of the Second World War, then in the Territorial Army, he was attached to the Royal Engineers at Hythe where he managed to rescue three soldiers of the East Kent Regiment who found themselves marooned in the middle of a minefield in which twelve of their comrades had been killed. He reached them by crawling along planks of wood which he carefully laid on the ground, one in front of the other, and managed to lead them back the way he had come. In recognition of his gallantry

The Matthews brewery at Wyke, Gillingham, Dorset in 1902. Beer was brewed here for over 200 years and their buffalo trademark was well known in the area.

he received the George Medal from King George VI.

Aunt Ina's face reminded me of a cushion – a much loved and sat upon cushion, providing and never failing to give comfort. She was a founder member of the Mother's Union (Onion, we called it). Although she came to like gin rather too much in her later years, she was as hard to beat at Bridge as she was at Croquet.

She had to put up with Uncle Blandford's philandering and got her revenge in harmless but subtle ways. Towards the end of his life when he was wheelchair bound following a stroke (he broke his neck twice out hunting), and clearly fancied the latest in a long line of nurses, Aunt Ina had the fading batteries on his electric wheelchair charged without telling him. She watched gleefully from the French windows in the drawing room when he took off unexpectedly fast over the rose garden to give corn to the peacocks and golden pheasants and ended up at the bottom of the ha-ha.

In 1773 the Matthews family owned a brewery in the small town of Gillingham in Dorset on the edge of the Blackmore Vale, west of Salisbury Plain and three miles or so from the Somerset border. They lived in The Old House in Milton on Stour and were soon to own the mill of that name when George Blandford Matthews married Charlotte Parham at the turn of the century. Charlotte came from Norrington Manor in Alvediston and had inherited a mill on a tributary of the Stour known as Purns Mill.

A mill on the Shreen Water is mentioned in the Domesday Book. At one time it was owned by Richard Perne who died in 1636 and it remained in his family for many generations. Rachel Perne, Richard's daughter, married Edward Rawson and they emigrated to Newburyport in the colony of Massachusetts, leaving behind a daughter also called Rachel whom they were never to see again. In 1650 Edward Rawson became Secretary of the Colony and he owned 6,000 acres of land. Among his descendants was William Howard Taft, President of the United States of America from 1909 to 1917.

The artist John Constable frequently stayed with the vicar of Gillingham, John Fisher, who was a close friend of Matthew Parham's, the miller at Purns, and Constable thought the mill enchanting and painted it four times.

Writing to his wife, Constable said of Gillingham:

'This is a melancholy place but it is beautifull, full of little bridges, rivulets, mills and cottage and the most beautifull trees and verdure I ever saw. The poor people are dirty and to approach one of the cottages is allmost insufferable'.

In 1825 Fisher wrote to Constable:

'The news is that Mat Parham's mill is burnt to the ground and exists only on your canvas. A huge, mis-shapen, new, bright, brick, modern, improved, patent monster is starting up in its stead.'

To this Constable replied:

'I am vexed at the fate of the poor old mill. There will soon be an end to the picturesque in the kingdom.' *

*From Constable's Correspondence, A.B. Beckett, Suffolk Record Society 1985

In fact, the Victorian building of 1830 was pleasing when I was young, being for the most part built of the same grey stone as the back wing of the charming mill house next door. The view that Constable painted from the millpond across the water meadows to Mere church with the Wiltshire downs beyond is unaltered. His broad-leaved riverside plants and rushes in the foreground still grow there. Many letters were exchanged over the years between Constable and Fisher, who subsequently became Archdeacon of Salisbury Cathedral, and many refer to Perne's Mill or Parham's Mill or simply the mill at Gillingham, now called Purns Mill.

In 2002, as I write, Purns Mill is still privately owned and run as an animal feed business by George Blandford Matthews's great-great-grandson, my brother, Pip. The brewery at Wyke is now an antiques warehouse and gallery and is owned and run by Camilla Parker Bowles' sister, Annabel Eliot.

THE FLIGHT

My mother was missing us out there in the tropics under the punkahs and the pink gins. So she arranged for us to fly out to Rangoon early in the new year, and the Burmah Oil Company were to pay our fares one way. The journey was to take two days and two nights in a six-engined Argonaut. We were to depart from London Airport and from there we would land at Rome, Cairo, Basra, Karachi, Bombay, Calcutta and, finally, Rangoon where our parents were to meet us. I was nine years old and Pip was six. The year was 1950.

We arrived hours early at London Airport on the day of departure. Granny had a bad cold and so Aunt Pam saw us off. She gave permission for photographs to be taken of Pip and me which the Airways wanted to used for publicity purposes with the slogan: 'Trust your children to the B.O.A.C.'

We wore matching Harris tweed coats and hats and gloves, and stood hand in hand on the runway in front of the silver, many-propellered aeroplane. We said goodbye and were handed over to the stewardess whom I decided I must like and so clung to her hand as we climbed up the steps and in through the door.

Granny had organised with much care and forethought two little baskets containing a wrapped present for each of us to open at the appropriate stopping place. They bore labels saying, 'To Darling Susie, open this at Cairo, with love from Granny.' Pip opened all his presents between London and Rome where my nice stewardess disappeared and was replaced by another. I felt immediately insecure and not a little afraid of what was to come. I did not think that my small brother understood what was going on. I felt better after I succeeded in herding him and most of his presents out of the aircraft along what seemed like miles of corridor through Customs and Immigration.

I held Pip firmly by the hand, the other clutching our passports, and we sat on a bench feeling weary and forlorn for what seemed a long time. Then we were herded back on to the aeroplane and slept during the flight to Cairo. We awoke to see the pyramids and the sphinx in the desert below. Whenever we landed we had to leave the aircraft for several hours, even if it was in the middle of the night and the journey seemed to us to have a lot of night in it. The stewardess disappeared again and was replaced by another. We were startled to see men swathed from head to toe in white robes with cords around their heads and their eyes seemed so black and their teeth so white in their dark-skinned faces. At Basra we trooped off once again into the desolate airport building.

After leaving Karachi we saw far below us the thick green treetops stretching away to the horizon. We realised it was the jungle and Pip began to cry at the thought of poisonous snakes and lions and tigers. In Bombay we were driven in a bus through the Gateway to India and along the smarter shopping streets and back to the airport. However, I did see the beggars propped up against the buildings, lying on the pavements where they lived and saw that some had no arms or only a stump for a leg, and all held out their hands to passers-by. Even the small children were begging. I was very shocked.

We arrived at Mingaladon Airport, Rangoon at 7 o'clock in the morning. My mother had ordered an early breakfast and she and our father were driven to the aerodrome where they saw the huge aeroplane land. Two small children slowly came down the steps still wearing the matching Harris tweed coats, hats and gloves they had left London in, and the temperature was well over 100 degrees. Pip saw Mummy and gave her a huge smile. 'Hello Auntie Pam!' he cried, whereupon she burst into tears.

RANGOON

Burrah Sahibs like my father lived in what were always known as Bungalows, but Greenbank was no bungalow. It was a stuccoed two-storied mansion.

Standing guard at the gate as we drove in was the Dirwan, who was a low-caste Indian guard. In front of the house were circular flower beds filled with red and yellow Cannas in a large lawn, and massed along the walls were strong smelling Petunias. Lined up to greet us were the main house servants: Bah Sin was the Burmese butler, who was much respected by the other servants. He wore voluminous white trousers with a maroon cummerbund at the waist and a white turban wrapped around his head. The Bearer was his Number Two, and Sammy, an Indian, was the Kitmegar, or manservant. Each Memsahib was expected to run a household of at least ten servants, and I soon met the Sweeper and the Pani Wallah, the Dirzhi and the Dhobi who did the laundry, Cook and his Boys and the Gardeners, or

Greenbank, Rangoon

Mahlis. A rigid caste system defined and restricted the tasks of each servant. The house servants considered themselves to be superior. It was generally believed among the Europeans that the Burmese were more trustworthy than the Indians. Some of them were Christians.

The rooms inside were marble floored, and punkahs whirled softly in the high ceilings. The walls were white and flecked with tiny lizards which were fondly treated as they lived on the mosquitoes which were a particular menace as Greenbank was built on the shores of a lake. Windows with cane blinds looked out over Jacaranda trees and Banana palms, Mimosa, Magnolia, Gardenia, Stephanotis and Bougainvillea and Mango trees with yellow and brown Orchids sprouting from the trunks and branches. Windows with cane blinds looked out over the garden at the back where the lawn sloped down to the water's edge. The spiky grass was constantly watered and was interspersed with 'sensitive plants' which had tiny fern-like leaves which folded shut when touched. Next to the hard tennis court down by the lake was a clinker-built, English-looking boat tied to a jetty. Pip and I spent long hours every day pottering about in the boat. I learnt to do back dives off the side, and Pip managed to row with oars so long and heavy he had to stand up and push and pull with all his weight as he walked up and down. He wore a black rubber tyre around his tummy as he had not learnt to swim properly. Sometimes we saw the head of a water-snake leaving a tell-tale V trail of disturbance on the smooth surface, the sleek head showing at the apex. Sometimes we found large black leeches gorging blood (quite painlessly) on our legs and they had to be burnt off with a cigarette. We were forbidden to row out far, and never anywhere near the island where the Communists lived. I imagined they were like the Cannibals that Robinson Crusoe was so in fear of.

By day we always wore topees outside to protect our heads from the sun. We were sometimes troubled by prickly heat and we slept in beds entirely surrounded by a cage of mosquito netting. Many other English children had arrived in Rangoon by that time, and we were quickly sucked into a life of parties and picnics.

It was a life of leisure for my mother. Every morning Cook would come to her to discuss menus for the day, and he would organise the shopping in the market. Occasionally my mother would go into the kitchen quarters to inspect them for cleanliness. The servants lived in huts in a compound at the back of the house over which hung a perpetual cloud of curry smells. I loved to eat rice with them, dipping chillies in dahl and chewing beetle nut and spitting out the bitter red juice. We ate fruit from the garden which smelt and tasted of the sun; mangoes, lychees, cape gooseberries, paw-paw and pineapple, bananas, oranges and lemons.

My mother had been told by a friend that the salt loss can be so great in children through sweating in the intense heat of the tropics that to compensate, she must add a teaspoonful to our diet every day. At the end of lunch therefore, she gave Pip and me a small tumbler of water to drink with the salt added. We were both instantaneously very sick. Bah Sin was summoned and he sent for the Pani Wallah who surveyed the mess on the marble floor, shook his head and said it was definitely the Sweeper's job to clean it up. The Sweeper had gone to the market so there it had to remain until he returned. Pani Wallahs were becoming redundant and were therefore rather lazy. Ten years previously their tasks had been important: to provide water everywhere in the house for washing, drinking and for toilet purposes, but now that there was efficient, though crude, plumbing in most European houses his importance had diminished.

A stream of travelling salesmen would arrive at the house, strewing the lawn with their wares. Out of large shabby suitcases would pour lengths of exquisite silks and cottons, all locally woven, or primitive paintings, relics from the war, carpets, shoes or beads and bracelets. Some were old Naga warriors from the hills with ivory rings through their noses and fearsome facial scars, and some were tribesmen from Tibet or Karens from the north.

At night jackals howled and crickets chirped. Starving pi-dogs, goats and sacred white cows lay about in the streets by day lulled by the constant noise of tinkling bells from the bullock carts, rickshaws and tongas and the smell of rotting fruit and vegetables. The Irrawaddy delta was an area of vast paddy fields, worked by water buffalo with wide curling horns, belly deep in mud. I had a permanent and terrible fear of snakes, imagining them

43

ever near coiled in the shade of a bush, or in a dark corner in the house especially after my father found a cobra in a cupboard and shot it.

The Shwe Dagon pagoda dominated Rangoon with its gold leafed dome which shone by day reflecting the sun, and by night reflecting the moon. The many steps up to it were stained red with beetle nut juice. Once inside everyone took off their shoes. Inside it was very dark with a series of small shrines each with its own benign Buddha including one enormous reclining Buddha painted gold with emerald eyes. The hands of the real Buddha were in the pagoda and pilgrims came from all over the east to worship there. My mother told us that she considered Buddha to be a Disciple of God, as was Jesus, and she explained about the Buddhist belief in reincarnation which I found more plausible than going up in the sky to Heaven.

There were a great many rickshaws pulled by coolies with lungis tucked up between their legs and bare feet. Daddy told us of the drunken evenings spent in the main square when he and his friends used to put ten rupees each in the kitty, and then take over several rickshaws, put the driver in the back and tear off round the square, pulling the rickshaws behind them. The first one back to the Silver Grill got the loot.

My father was driven to his office in the centre of the town at 6.00 a.m. and returned for lunch and a rest through the hottest hours of the day. There was no air conditioning. Then he went back to work until 7 o'clock. He played a lot of golf and was the Burma Champion. His handicap was one. There were horse races and yachting on the lake, and tennis and swimming at Kokine, the European club. Shooting parties went up country and camped for days on end. Daddy was bitten by a dog on the golf course when we were there and had to have twenty painful anti-rabies injections in his stomach.

Pip and I were given two black Minah birds in a cage by a Chinese family we were friends with. The birds never learnt to speak English and I felt sorry for them and wanted to let them fly free. I do not think they spoke Chinese either.

The Burmese women had faultless bone structure and a graceful carriage. They wore transparent blouses with glass fastenings on top of the lungi which was an open-ended skirt wound round them. They combed their hair with coconut oil and wore it coiled up on top of their heads. Years later, my father told me they did not have any pubic hair.

The months passed and my mother decided to start a regime of lessons. With the help of the Pears Encyclopaedia, she taught us all the rivers and capital cities of the world. While engrossed in the geography lesson she would look up to find Pip's seat empty. He had slunk out of the room and was usually to be seen pushing the boat out on the lake. Reading came late to Pip. He wrote 'b' for 'd' and said 'feith' for 'thief' and 'fly-ashes' when he meant 'eye-lashes'. Dyslexia was an unknown word in those days but it was to hold him back.

One night in Digboi, Assam, we were woken up and snatched from our beds to be taken downstairs on to the lawn where we gazed, horrified, up at the house to see it shaking, as was the ground beneath our feet. It was a severe earth tremor and we were to experience several more, but I do not remember any in Rangoon.

It was said that my brother was accident prone and two particular accidents come to mind. In Digboi, we were both leaning over the balcony at the top of the stairs trying to eavesdrop on the grown-ups when Pip toppled right over and crash landed on to the marble floor below. Half an hour later, still concussed and wrapped in a blanket in the ambulance with my mother, he suddenly sat up and said he was hungry so she told the driver to turn round and go home for tea.

Another drama occurred when, at the end of the war, my mother decided to take us to England for the first time. We were to sail on the Bibby Line ship, the S.S. Georgic, and before we left my father gave a farewell party on the platform of the station in Calcutta. Surrounded by merry laughter and lots of legs I soon realised that my little brother was nowhere to be seen. I saw people shouting and pointing down to the railway

46

line beneath the carriages of the train which was to leave for Bombay where we were to embark. I quickly slipped through the throng of noisy friends until I found my mother and tugged very hard at her dress:

'Pip is under the train!' I shouted.

'Under the train? Don't be silly, darling!' she said.

'He is, he is,' I cried, jumping up and down.

She ran over with my father in tow to where a crowd had gathered and were pointing into the gloom between the platform and the carriages. My father ran up to the engine and told the driver that on no account was he to move the train because his son was lying on the track. It was not an easy task to get to Pip and, after much shouting in Hindustani, a suitably small and thin Indian was found and sent down on to the railway line under the carriages. When Pip was carried out he was semi-conscious and covered in blood from a badly cut chin.

My mother thought it a good idea for Pip to stay on in Rangoon. I was to fly home alone to England and Granny and go to boarding school. At my farewell party at the Kokine Swimming Club I slipped as I ran along the high diving board, which was covered with hessian, and fell cutting my forehead. My father dived into the pool with his clothes on to rescue me. I had to have stitches and a large plaster for the long flight home. It was unclear whether, in our excitement in racing to be the first to dive in, Pip might have pushed me.

LESSONS

Granny met me at London Airport when I arrived back from Rangoon. We spent the night at the V.A.D. Club in Cumberland Place where she told me that Miss Lever, our Dutch governess, had not returned from Holland and that I was to go to boarding school. I felt a great loss at this, my first taste of betrayal, for Mee-Lee had told me she would never leave us.

The following day Granny and I went to Peter Jones in Sloane Square to buy my uniform. We took the underground and Granny got out at Charing Cross to change to the Northern Line and I did not. The door clanged shut in my face as I hurried to follow her and I hurtled on quite alone. A fellow passenger saw my terror and realising what had happened, she got out with me at the next station where we waited hoping that Granny would be on the next train which she was. I was then, and still am, nervous of the top step of an elevator, or moving staircase as Granny called it, and make an exaggerated leap across the jaws at the top and bottom.

Steeped in girls' school literature and the colourful accounts of my mother's career at Westonbirt, I was eager to go to boarding school. The Hall School, perched on a lonely Somerset hilltop moated, turreted and partially surrounded by a high stone wall, was more Colditz Castle than the exclusive Westonbirt. Its prospectus appealed to my mother with photographs of bare-footed girls in tunics on the lawn doing Dalcroze, which was movement to music. With its accent on religious toleration, the arts and crafts and an abhorrence of any form of elitism, it offered an education somewhat different to that which she had known. I suspect that my mother was a closet socialist. She could not bear any form of show, but I was not a shy child and liked being the centre of attention. How it must have irked her.

Miss Brooks, my headmistress, was a Quaker. Tall, thin and elegant, she liked her girls to be feminine with a broad-based education which would equip them well in whatever circumstances they might find themselves. She did not suffer fools gladly and the less bright were neglected. Talent, whether artistic or academic, she nurtured. As the school was situated in the depths of the country, first-rate teaching staff were difficult to attract. It was her personality alone which lit the fires of creativity in her pupils and made them aware of the spiritual rewards in life.

As juniors (I was nine years old), we had to go to bed at 6.30 p.m. This was to relieve pressure on the staff. The dormitory was called The Blue Room and beside each narrow bed was a blue-painted bedside table upon which we were allowed a framed photograph. The thin mattresses were full of lumps which could be picked up and rearranged. We each had a toy animal to sleep with and mine was the *Daily Mail* character with a long nose, Flook. There were several golliwogs and teddy bears.

We were taught to make our beds with hospital corners. I was a light sleeper and awoke when anyone coughed or went out to the lavatory. My chief pleasure was reading by torchlight under the bedclothes.

There was very often a particularly horrible smell in the loo where on a hook were torn out pages of *Women's Own* magazines which I would take down and avidly read. I thought it kind of Matron to have put them there, but, of course, their purpose was quite different. After several weeks I decided to open one of the smelly bundles wrapped up in the paper and placed in a closed bin beside the lavatory. I was shocked to see the blood. I knew nothing about menstruation, nothing about how babies came.

Two of my friends met with scant approval from Granny. One was the daughter of a draper whose small shop was in Bridport and the other was Jewish. This snobbery was only lightly touched upon, and a few years later I was to understand the inbred class structure which smothered the countryside like a vast cobweb. My mother's family were 'trade', but brewers were thought to be more socially acceptable than doctors, dentists or the high street merchants. Despite their money, it was still considered, after more than a hundred years, new money, and the landed gentry on the shelf above closed their ranks protectively around themselves.

We were very interested in our burgeoning bodies and longed to have something to put into a bra, but we were critical of one another and I remember an unkind song we made up to taunt Jane Wilkes beginning, 'Does your bust hang low, can you swing it to and fro?'

Susan Hedges had alarming attacks of asthma in our dormitory. She had to sit up all night trying to breathe. Towards the end of term she had to be rushed to hospital in Yeovil where she died.

When I was thirteen Miss Brooks spoke to me in her study and said that I was a Born Leader but really must try to lead in the right direction. She was, nevertheless, putting me in a small dormitory with poor Penny Monkton who had something called epilepsy and that I must behave in a responsible and sensible manner when she had a fit. Soon afterwards I was there when she had a grand mal attack and got someone to run for Matron while I held her head as I had been shown, taking care that she did not swallow her tongue. She thrashed about foaming at the mouth and wetting her pants. She wanted to be a surgeon when she grew up, an ambition I don't suppose she was able to achieve.

I remember feeling hungry nearly all the time at school and implored Granny to complain about the poor food. This she did, and Miss Brooks responded with an imperious sweep of the hand:

'Look at my girls,' she said, 'not one of them has acne.' The subject was changed.

At Westonbirt, girls had been known to arrive with their lady's maids who were lodged in the gatehouse. In my mother's day, some girls brought their ponies which they hunted with the Beaufort, and others their golf clubs as the school had an eighteen hole course in the grounds. Lying in bed in the dormitory on her first night, having brought none of these things, my mother was grilled by the others, which turned out to be an initiation ceremony for all new girls.

'How many bedrooms has your house got?' she was asked.

Feeling rather homesick, and not wanting to dwell upon dear old Castle House, my mother nonetheless quickly counted all the upstairs rooms she could think of, including the linen room and attics, and answered 'ten'. That seemed to be fairly acceptable and was followed by another question. 'How long is your drive?' and then, 'How many horses have you?' After a time my mother settled down, but disaster struck two of her greatest friends before the year was out. Rosalind Ducat Hamilton threw herself off the music room balcony for love of her housemistress, Claire Fitzherbert, and broke her ankle. She was afterwards taken away and sent abroad to school. Charlotte Fane was expelled for being caught drinking Black Velvets in the Cat & Custard Pot in the village.

The peak of my mother's career at Westonbirt was when she got into the cricket team, a feat achieved by showing extraordinary keenness before breakfast. She was to be seen throwing a cricket ball back and forth to Penelope Plunket in order to harden their hands.

Her sister, Pam, meanwhile was at Sherborne where her cousin, Jean Stratton, was Head Girl. Poor-Pam was very unhappy there, but she too knew some moments of glory when, besieged by junior girls who had crushes on her glamorous cousin, she offered to go into Jean's study bedroom and get hold of strands of hair from her brush which she would afterwards swap for tuck.

Granny and I had been to the Open Day at The Hall School the summer before I went to Burma. I had been enchanted by the play, 'The Selfish Giant', which was performed on the lawn with a backdrop of lupins and delphiniums. I was, later on, to be the youngest member of the cast of 'The Boy With The Cart' which was performed in London. I was the young Saint Francis in *'Saint Francis of Assisi'* which we did every night for a week at the Octagon Theatre in Bath. I also took part in a Dalcroze display in London, beating two-time with my left arm and three-time with my right, while my feet had to do something quite different. The school put on art exhibitions, concerts and ballet and country dance displays. I discovered that it was through dancing that I could most easily and naturally express my deepest emotions, and in ballet that I found a challenge and a discipline and an ecstasy of expression which I had not known.

Granny moved house again. This time to a 17th century farmhouse in Kingston Deverill, a village so named because King Alfred had rolled a boulder down the hillside saying, 'Where this rests I shall build a camp' – thus, the King's stone, under the hill. The village was surrounded by dramatic downland scenery. One dented hillside was called, appropriately, Dame's Bottom.

I said that I should like a pony for my tenth birthday, and so on the morning of December 23rd, a blue horsebox delivered to the door a small bay New Forest filly complete with saddle, bridle and grooming kit. Thereafter I was more often mounted than not. With a boy called Clive from the village, who also had a pony, we would vanish for the entire day, roaming the downs, collecting birds' eggs. I boasted to girls at school that from the top of Mere Down the land belonged to one uncle or another for as far as the eye could see, and that claim was, and still is, very nearly true.

Greta Phillips was a lonely, fey widow who lived in the village with whom I spent many happy hours. She was obsessed with horses despite having lost her only child, a ten-year-old daughter, in an accident when she was thrown on to the road by her frightened pony. Mrs Phillips taught me how to ride with 'quiet hands, no visible aids, just instinctive communication between you and your pony'.

A Roman road ran in an almost straight line across the top of the downs. It was originally constructed from Salisbury to Bath and in places the flint paving stones could be clearly seen. Mrs Phillips told me she had heard the sound of a coach-and-four approaching one misty morning along the Roman road. Her horse had tensed and shied up on to the bank as the phantom passed by and rattled on into the distance. She later discovered that a coach had regularly plied between Sarum and Bath a hundred years ago and passed over Mere Down at the very time she had been riding there.

Anne Bullen was a friend of Greta's and when she was asked to organise a riding display for the Horse of the Year Show at Haringey in London in 1954, I was chosen to represent the South & West Wilts Pony Club. We enacted a scene from Jorrocks with hounds (beagles) meeting at the Cat & Fiddle. Following a trail of aniseed they set off in full cry around the ring with twenty children following on their ponies dressed in period costume designed by Anne Bullen. Five-year-old Sarah Bullen got loud applause when she cantered in side-saddle on a Shetland pony wearing a peacock blue velvet habit with an ostrich feather in her hat. My pony, Firelight, usually refused at the brush fence and there was little I could do about it. We were there for a week with two performances a day with some in front of members of the Royal Family and we were on television.

For a Christmas treat which included my mother's and my December birthdays, we used to travel up to London by train from Gillingham to Waterloo. We went to Bertram Mills' Circus where I was fascinated by the performing fleas which were harnessed to chariots and ran races and then we went to Peter Pan. I believed so much in the fairies that I clapped until my hands hurt so that poor Tinkerbell should live and not die. We once went to *Salad Days* by Julian Slade and afterwards I wanted to become an actress and sing and dance my heart out on the stage.

Just outside Basingstoke I gazed out of the train window in order not to miss the massive sign which proclaimed: 'YOU ARE NOW IN STRONG COUNTRY'. It was an advertisement for ale and I thought that for people who did not know what real country looked like, to have a placard like that stuck up among the squalid outskirts of a large town, seemed to me very misleading. Approaching Waterloo I remember taking in every detail of the black-backed terrace houses lining the track and thought them the most dismal, depressing slums I had ever seen. I wondered why the people living in them did not simply run away to the country and eat turnips and blackberries and shelter in a hole in a haystack.

When first I saw the English countryside from a train window I was four years old. We had arrived by ship in Liverpool from Bombay. We left the city and were travelling south towards Westbury in Wiltshire,

'Why', I asked, 'didn't you tell me that England is all a garden?'

THE MILL

Purns Mill House is built astride the river which, in living memory, has never flooded. The back section of the house is of ancient stone and was clearly part of the original mill on the Shreen water, a tributary of the Stour. The front is late Georgian. The garden is a small island with a feed stream to the millpond curling round to join the main river at the bottom of the tennis court. As the millers prospered over the centuries they altered the house to suit their lifestyle.

During the war my grandmother let the house to Sir Robert and Lady Sutton who covered the walls with five large Gainsborough paintings of ancestors including The Blue Boy. These pictures were 'entailed', a word I heard used to explain the Sutton's seemingly impoverished state. I remained mystified for some time and remember giving the couple my close scrutiny. In summer, Sir Robert, wearing shabby khaki shorts and chuplee sandals, pottered about the garden digging up plantains in

Purns Mill House

the lawn with a George II three-pronged fork, a dilapidated trug hooked over one arm. Lady Sutton occupied
the roof of the house in hot weather and sunbathed in
the nude, to the delight of the mill men eating their
elevenses on top of the nearby cake-store. One day in
the autumn of 1956 Granny drove Pip and me over to
the mill. She told us our parents were leaving Burma and
coming to live at Purns Mill. I remember gazing at the
untidy garden and the handsome house, and hearing
the constant noise of the river.

When we came to live at Purns the mill was a large
horseshoe of grey stone with an arch in the centre with
a way through to the deep millpond. To my eyes it
was both beautiful and alluring, although this was the

Victorian rebuild. The pond was artificially dredged annually and the water was deep enough for us to dive off the bridge. We had a boat and later a canoe on the river. The water level was controlled by the use of hatches which were raised and lowered by turning heavy iron wheels. The river was home to ducks, kingfishers, otters and water rats. My father planted cricket bat willows along the banks intending to harvest them at ten-year intervals. The cows ate all except three. At the back of the mill was an eel trap. Early on in the century there had been a thriving market in eels, and with the right conditions, which included a full moon, as many as fifty were caught at one time in the grill. They travelled overland if necessary and, with the determination of salmon, they overcame any obstacle in order to reach their spawning grounds. They then returned to the sea – the Caribbean Sargasso sea.

The force of the water as it cascaded down huge stone steps to the undershot mill wheel made a deafening roar and the walls there were covered with lichen and ferns. The river flows past the mill buildings and under the mill house and through the garden. Trout were put in every few years, but in spate they were carried down past our land to the benefit of the Gillingham Angling Association. In those days there was no septic tank for the house and we sometimes flushed the loos simultaneously and played pooh-sticks.

Purns Mill 1960

One wing of the mill used to be stables and coach houses. The rest of it was a series of vast grain stores on four levels with perfect wooden floors polished by a thin coating of barley meal. Large stones ground the grain, one turning on the other as had been the method for hundreds of years. A mill is mentioned on the Shreen water at Gillingham in the county of Dorset in the Doomsday Book.

Two hundred weight hessian sacks were used in those days. The sacks were tied with twine and a system of trap doors opened and closed behind them when they were hoisted up to the required floor level. This was done by looping a chain over the top of the sack and then pulling a rope which started an electric hoist mechanism. Pip used to pretend to be a sack and make me operate the rope. I watched speechless with admiration as he disappeared into the upper reaches of the building. The mill was a labyrinth of stores which were ideal for playing hide and seek, sardines and murder. We had a huge advantage over any other children who came to play as we knew every last corner of it, taught by the hungry cats who controlled the rat population. Our greatest treat was to go with Syd or Charlie on the lorries delivering layer's mash, sow & weaner nuts, horse and pony feed or cowcake to the farms.

Several years later, after the mill had begun to manufacture its own feed on a large scale, the molasses tank overflowed into the river. Someone downstream noticed something thick and black floating on top of the water and alerted the Water Board who rang the mill demanding to know what foul substance had polluted the river Stour. Upon being told that some molasses had unfortunately escaped into the river the Water Board official ordered the river to be pumped dry at once. An hour later four huge lorries with pumping gear and arc lights rampaged over the lawns and flower beds. They succeeded not only in pumping the river dry but also managed to kill all the trout. The mill was inoperative for a week and officials were deaf to the explanation that molasses was black treacle, not oil, and was used in the manufacture of cowcake and unlikely to kill fish or anything else.

The river sang me to sleep as it ran directly under my bedroom, two floors down. Its soft, busy gurgle on its fifty-mile journey to the sea was the last thing I heard at night and, along with the peacocks at the Kendalls and my bantam cocks in the yard, it was the first sound I heard in the morning.

We had help in the house and we never had to make our beds. Until I married I was under the impression that baths simply cleaned themselves when the water was let out. I do not remember ever having to do anything I did not want to do. I rode my pony, Firelight, and Pip went up the river for hours with his air gun and our beloved Labrador, Smitch. He once shot a snipe flying and Uncle Blandford wrote to *The Field* describing this remarkable feat.

A few miles away was the National Stud and the horses were fed special oats from Canada. Peter Burrell ran the stud in those days and used to let my father know when the Queen was expected to come down to see her stallion, Big Game. I rode down there one day and a large black car was forced to a walking pace in the narrow lane. When it had room to pass the Queen smiled up at me and said, 'What a nice pony!'

We loved to go on scavenging hunts with patient mothers at the wheels of the cars. The first home after completing the lists of things to do got the prize. Example: 'What colour pyjamas is the East Knoyle postman wearing this week?' 'Bring back a hoof-pick, a blue beret and a Matthews & Co. beer mat.' Sometimes the clues were in rhyme.

I remember being aware, young as I was, that I was most fortunate and privileged. No wonder Pip was unhappy at prep school near Camberley and that he ran away several times. I did once from The Hall School and got as far as the bottom of the drive before I changed my mind and went back up the hill.

In 1952 Granny sent a telegram to my father in Burma saying she was being advised (by Uncle Blandford) to sell the family milling business, G.B. Matthews & Co., of which she was Chairman, unless my father was prepared to return to the U.K., run it and live in the mill house. Dad had just been promoted in the Burmah Oil Company and told to go to the London headquarters in Britannic House. We, no doubt, would have found ourselves living a very different life in Chertsey or Sunningdale had he not accepted Granny's offer.

Granny was only forty when her husband, Arthur

Pip and Switch

Matthews, died suddenly leaving her with three teenaged children. When in the First World War, where he was Mentioned in Despatches, he fell ill and was operated on in a Field Hospital in France. The removal of his appendix was not competently done and this was to kill him in the form of peritonitis some years later. Granny was grief-stricken and for comfort had to share her bed with her sister, Marjorie, for several weeks until she felt stronger. In time, she became very involved in public service. She was on numerous committees, a Magistrate for thirty years, a Governor of schools and a Borstal. Both her parents had been awarded the O.B.E. and her father, Arthur White, was a Deputy Lieutenant of Wiltshire.

I am fairly certain that my grandmother never entered a bank in her life. I remember her ringing up the branch manager in Mere asking him to have a glass or two of sherry with her before lunch and would he please bring her five pounds. I suppose she must have had a chequebook at some stage but I never saw it. She was very clothes conscious and trips to Jolly's in Bath with my mother proved tiring because Granny suffered from the family disease of alternitivitis. Everything she bought had to be brought home or sent On Approval. All one summer, nearly everyone who came in through her front door was asked what colour they thought the hall walls should be painted. Their choices were so varied that

Granny became 'quite muddled' and so no decorating could be carried out that year.

Between the two world wars Granny lost her pearl necklace on the Paris to Nice sleeper. I cannot think why she took it off when she went to bed. She had a habit of twiddling the real pearls around her right index finger and if, on a rare occasion, she was not wearing them, her hair would be brought into play and worked into a knot from which her finger was hard to extract. Knotted pearls would be uncomfortable to sleep with.

Granny would tell me stories of her mother, Minnie Beauchamp White, as a young wife living at Charnage. She would write to her mother, Fanny, at Norton Hall in Midsomer Norton near Bath, every day. Quite often, if the postman arrived to collect the letter and she had not finished writing it, she would ask him to go into the kitchen and have a cup of tea and wait until she had.

Granny gave me for safekeeping two letters she had written to her parents when staying with her Grand-mother, Fanny, in 1903. They are beautifully written. She was ten years old. This one was written from The Grange, Midsomer Norton:

'Dear Mother & Father,
I know you wont mind me writing in pencil. I think if you saw me now you would not believe it was me for I am hardly a bit yellow (*she must have had jaundice.*)

My parents at Stourton, 1940

The drive down must have taken it away, I did enjoy it
so. We waited a little in Mere to get a paper and some
orange slices (but they turned out to be lemon) and then
we went on. I don't think Uncle Willie's mangle hauling
was as bad as yours, Father, as I did not see so much
mud on the whole journey as much as is in our lane. We
saw Stourton House. It is nearly built up, I think. I think
it very pretty. What a lot of lodges it has. I think the
prettiest thing I saw on the drive was the Witham
woods. They are sweet, all the different leaves and the
lovely tall trees and the stumps growing up between and
then when the trees were too close together that you
could not see in between, every now and then came a

path with the sun shining on the dewy grass. It was lovely, how you would enjoy it. We went through a lot of pretty villages which I cannot remember but I think Kilmerston a sweetly pretty place and the church is very nice. I began to eat my sandwiches before Tweks Hill. They were lovely. I like that place very much. Then we got to Nunney. What an old Castle there is there, so ivy-grown and pretty. After we had just got out of Nunney Grannie had a biscuit and her brandy and water and I had my cake and all the milk. I have forgotten all that went by next till we got to Wotbury. It is a lovely place. Grannie says the clergyman Mr Witaker used to teach you Mother. Grannie told me where her Doctor lived. I saw such a funny thing there. It was a sort of gig driven by two black ponies one in front of the other. Then we got to Vobster where you were born, Mother, and I saw the house where Grandpa lived. I also saw the house where Uncle Frank was taken when he was six weeks old. I think Vobster a sweet place. Then we got to Almerston. I think I remember that. We got home to The Grange at quarter to four. I am having a very nice time. Grannie is getting up. I have only just. They are cutting up the tree, they burst it yesterday. Auntie Blanche and Auntie Janet came down just as we got here and they quite cheered Grannie up. Perhaps when you have done with this letter Miss Thatcher might like to see it. Heaps of love to both and 9,000,000,000 of kisses,

Yours ever, Gladys.

P.S. I am going to make Baby a rag scrapbook while I am here. Out in the field opposite Uncle Louie has a lot of horned sheep and a lot of little lambs. Is it not early for them? Do horned sheep have these lambs sooner than ours?'

Granny told me she had got used to being centre stage for much of her life. As she became older she realised she had been relegated to the wings, observing and listening. She did not want to die because she so wanted to know what happened next.

Granny looked after herself well and her hair and nails were done the day before she died aged 86 on the 2nd August 1979. She died of cancer in Pam's house in Blewbury. I slept on the floor in the bathroom next to her bedroom and was glad to have been there at the end with a gentle Macmillan nurse reading to her from the Bible. She had left instructions for her coffin to be draped in the flag of the British Legion and it was then to be taken from Mere church to the cemetery on a bier. Frank's son-in-law, Woods, blew the Last Post on his bugle as she was laid to rest in the same grave as her husband and next to her parents.

MADEMOISELLE

My mother felt I should have a stepping stone after leaving school and before living in London. A levels were not encouraged and university for girls hardly talked about. Blue stockings did exist in the wider family but they tended to have an aura of weirdness about them. She ruled out the possibility of a Season for me: 'What would be the point in all that expense since you will be invited to the coming-out dances of your friends anyway?' Had I been shy, fat or gauche my mother may have thought differently. Instead I was sent for a year to a Finishing School in Versailles, just outside Paris.

Mademoiselle Voellmey, stolid and grasping, provided a basic grounding in French history and manners. We, twelve girls in all, learned how to eat a banana with a knife and fork, how to ascend and descend a flight of stairs in a long skirt and how to step out of a taxi without showing too much leg. We were taken to dress shows at the couture houses in Paris and I put my name down for Scottish Country Dancing at the Sorbonne. I had been told by my friends, the Couret twins, that 'plaid' was all the rage and the attractive men were thither bound. We had lessons in cookery (not a word of English was allowed), but we were kept on short rations at meal times. I remember buying a bar of chocolate and stuffing it in a baguette and eating the whole lot. I went to ballet classes where there were a few boys as well as girls. I wore what I thought was a sexy black wrap-over top and black tights. We played tennis on a covered court which was close to a S.H.A.P.E., base (Supreme Head-quarters Allied Powers Europe). This acted as a magnet to a couple of my friends. We used to wander around the gardens and grounds of the Palace of Versailles and the Petit Trianon but we were not allowed to go on the Metro unless accompanied by a member of staff. Mademoiselle Voellmey said we might be in danger from the white slave traffic and that an English girl had been drugged by injection and bundled out of a carriage on the metro and never seen again.

In my letters home I complained that we were only allowed two baths a week in water no deeper than a line painted on the side three inches up in red nail varnish. My best friend was called Erika. Pert and pretty, she was also seventeen, German, but spoke fluent English. All I knew about her background was that her father was dead and the family lived in Baden-Baden. Erika told me that if I made up my eyes (which were fringed with blonde lashes) I could turn myself into a beauty. She taught me the mysteries of make-up and from then on it seemed to me that I grew into my face. I was thrilled when Erika invited me to Germany to stay with her during the summer holidays. When I told my father her surname, Von Brauschwitz, he was shocked and said he had been tried at Nuremberg for war crimes and didn't I realise that members of my family had been killed in two world wars? Of course, I did not go and it ended our friendship.

BAGGAGE

When my Murray grandmother came to stay in Dorset she sent her luggage in advance. The stationmaster would ring to say the trunk was in the waiting room and my mother, wound up with irritation and trepidation, would drive in her Morris Minor to collect it. A week later her mother-in-law would arrive along with Pat, an aged Scottish terrier whose nightcap was brandy and fudge, and her daughter, Esme, sweet-natured and pretty but wistfully described as 'wanting'. Her happiest time had been during the war when she enjoyed a brief fling with an American airman when she was stationed near Ipswich in the WAF. He was considered unsuitable.

In the early fifties my Great Aunt Jean Milne Murray came to stay. She arrived by train from Edinburgh where she lived alone in a large flat in Mardale Crescent. Unscrupulous people had taken advantage of her increasing senility and persuaded her to part with treasures and cheques. Aunt Jean's kitbag of war memories would have deeply shocked and silenced every one of them. She had nursed in and out of the trenches in France and was awarded the MBE amongst other medals. I have a long letter to her mother dated the 15th February 1917 in which she describes in detail the investiture at Buckingham Palace where she and Sister McLeod, who was in charge of the hospital ship, *St Andrew*, were the only two women among two hundred officers. They were chaperoned by Sir Arthur Leveson and The Hon. Charlotte Knollys and afterwards each had a private audience with Queen Alexandra at Marlborough House.

'The Queen was charming & looked charming & made me feel quite at home at once. I had quite a long time with her. She asked me all about the Tommies & spoke about our work & the maimed men and she seemed particularly interested in the blinded men. She told me about the hospitals for them in London & how they were trained to read & in various trades so that they can all be useful. She asked about our hospital & if we were comfortable. I told her how much we appreciated the fur capes she sent us and she was very pleased. Miss Knollys told me how deaf the Queen is but I seemed able to make her hear. I fancy she reads the lips, she seemed to watch very closely, in fact so closely that I couldn't look about the room at all. Really she was delightful and I enjoyed every minute.'

Jean goes on to describe how she went with friends to the St James' theatre that evening where they saw Sir George Alexander in *The Aristocrat*. She left the following day at 1.20 p.m. on the train from Charing Cross to return to the 20th General Hospital at Camiers in France.

In Dorset our dog, Smitch, sensed that our elderly visitor was vulnerable because he refused to leave Jean's side. One day, when she was left alone, she wandered out of the house and up the lane. My parents were frantic until some worrying hours later, the police rang to say 'a lady and a Labrador' had been found fourteen miles away in Wincanton. Both were being brought back to Purns Mill in a police van.

My maternal grandmother sometimes bought her clothes from Marshall & Snelgrove in London. These were always On Approval and arrived at the station in large flowered boxes. I wonder what one's emotional baggage would look like: a brown trunk made of fierce webbing trussed up with wooden bands, a black metal trunk with metal corners and a shiny padlock, or a battered leather trunk with a faded chintz lining and a drawer which lifts out?

In those days there was time to adjust, time to prepare, time to approve, time to despair, and time to get it over with.

END GAME

They have put her into sheltered housing
A little box of lonely walls
With no sharp edges or steps to trip her up;
She who has lived in ivory and igloo
In marble and mud hut – and never slipped,
Was trapped in limbo now.
Weather weary, she arranged herself
To wait and wait,
Head heavy with happenings
And feet travel sore
It was then that she caught in her tired gaze
A butterfly in a frenzy of flapping,
Trying to find a hold upon the red panic button
Beside the only door.

DOWNTOWN D.C.

I was eighteen when I caught the love disease, became besotted and deaf to reason and 'there are more fish in the sea' observations. As time went on and the object of my affection proved hard to catch, my obsession drove my parents to suggest I go far away across a vast ocean in order to get on with my life.

I was to encounter difficulties in getting a visa to work in the United States because I had been born in Burma. Their quota for the Burmese was full. My father had been born in India. I had therefore to arrange two fallbacks as I went up to the American Embassy in London to show them that my skin was white and my hair red. I had proof of my paternal grandfather's birth in Edinburgh and my sponsor in the States was to be a family friend, the Secretary of Commerce, Luther Hodges, who was number three under President Kennedy. This did the trick.

In 1961 I flew into Idlewild Airport, New York, and

went through Immigration where I had to give up my British passport and swear allegiance to the Flag. I was told the passport would be returned when I returned to the U.K. I assured the young immigration officer that I was very happy to be coming in to his country and he grinned and muttered, 'Gee, I wish we could have some more looking like you.'

I flew over the city in a helicopter to Newark and was mighty glad I was not going to have to take on New York. It looked terrifying. I went for a few weeks to stay with a family in West Virginia who lived in a house very like Tara in *Gone With the Wind*, but larger. The black cook, Hattie, was a forceful character. She wanted to know if English people also had to pay for their funerals before they died, as she did every month. She taught me how to make corn pudding and pecan pie. I went with Ben, one of the gardeners, to a drive-in cinema with a gigantic screen erected in a field. Ben was my age and going to university in the fall. After munching our way through hamburgers bought through the car window, and sipping Coke from a can, Ben turned and kissed me passionately. I would have been disappointed if he had not. I do not remember a thing about the film.

I flew to Washington D.C. to stay with an English friend and, using my secretarial skills, I wanted to find a job.

A month later I found myself gazing in awe at a huge

and beautiful building. It appeared to be all marble, outside and in, and turned out to be the home of the yellow *National Geographic* magazine. At the reception desk I asked to see the Personnel Manager and was told he did not see anybody without a prior appointment. I replied that I felt sure he would like to see me because I was English.

'We have two English girls in this building, Miss, and eight in our New York office,' came the reply.

Nevertheless, I did see him and told how I had been born in Burma, brought up in India, and educated in England and in France. I had got him interested. He said he would call a colleague down from the top floor to meet me because it so happened that he was working on an article about Burma and wanted to know how well I remembered that secret country. I was employed, and started the following week.

In a journal I kept at that time I describe a typical day:

Early morning in December 1962 at 2319 Virginia Avenue, Washington D.C., USA, an alarm clock shrieks. Two humps occupied two wooden beds, two clothes-strewn trunks lay upon bare floorboards. Dust rested delicately on the white venetian blind over the window and on scattered cosmetics set out on top of the chest of drawers. An arm reached out and switched on a small transistor radio whose voice presently filled the room . . .' and it is now 12 degrees in downtown areas, snow flurries are reported in Arlington, Virginia, which will probably spread into the City by noon. The temperature will drop tonight to zero in the suburbs and . . .'

'Susie, are we on the North Pole?' A hump materialised into a tousled, blue nylon-clad Judy.

'Thank goodness for the Buggy. I wouldn't go to work at all this morning if we didn't have a car, first day at a new job or not.' . . . 'and are bumper to bumper from Key Bridge, Maryland, to Connecticut and Pennsylvania Avenues . . .' the man on the wireless droned on, '. . . 15th and M streets are blocked by a breakdown and motorists are warned of icy conditions everywhere.'

My Revlon foundation cream had frozen, and Judy could not find her eyeliner brush. Instant coffee was made and Liz, the owner of the Buggy, announced that it was 8.15 and time to set off. She worked on Capitol Hill for Congressman Waggoner. We used to tease her about how long she took to say 'This is Congressman Waggoner's office' in her Southern drawl when we rang her office. Three scarved heads trooped out of the front door into the below freezing outside. Virginia Avenue crunched with the sound of snow-chained tyres, a continuous stream of commuting traffic was going past us up three lanes. Crossing the road to get to the Buggy was an art that required nerve, timing and pretty faces.

The Buggy was a dilapidated Volkswagen, sporting a virtually non-existent convertible hood.

'Please Buggy, start, start, start', Liz prayed, tugging at the choke. The Buggy did not start.

Nothing would induce the Buggy to start; Judy and I got out and pushed from the rear, only to get her front bumper enmeshed with that of a prosperous Buick. Judy announced that she was now a quarter of an hour late on her first day at a new job. Leaving Liz glaring at the snow-covered, forlorn-looking little car, Judy and I set off down 23rd Street on the thirty-minute walk to our offices.

'I can't even breathe, let alone see where I'm going,' I moaned as the wind bit into our faces.

'Now I know what it must have been like for Hilary, Tensing and our *Geographic* man on Everest.'

'What was the *Geographic* man doing?' Judy asked.

'Looking for the Yeti,' I answered proudly. 'I'm going to try walking backwards. Can't stand this wind on my skin.'

Someone had told me that redheads have one layer of skin less than the average person.

Exactly forty-five minutes late we entered our offices – mine with the National Geographic Society, and Judy with the *Washington Post* across the street. I hugged a radiator for half an hour, attempting to thaw out, and then sat down to finish typing the manuscript I had started the day before, 'Albatrosses in the Antarctic' by John Aldrich.

Judy joined me for lunch in the *Geographic* cafeteria. She had narrowly escaped being run over when crossing the road on a red light.

'You'll be an angel before you know it,' yelled a cab driver as he screeched to an abrupt halt at the crossing.

We sat eating a very good meal in the *Geographic* winter temperature of 80 degrees. It is an air conditioned 60 in summer. We discussed whether or not Judy would go back to the *Washington Post* which she said was simply awful, but in the end decided she would stick it out for the rest of the week.

After lunch we trudged out into the freezing atmosphere huddled up against the biting wind.

We entered the People's Drug Store where we bought earmuffs, green tights and Aspirin, and then went to Magruders, Washington's most exclusive food store, and intended to shock Denise when she saw the Magruder paper bags. (They don't give Green Stamps there and Denise collects them.) We bought more Metrecal, celery, Egg Nog and Banana yoghurt. Passing Erlebacher's we thought we might boost morales and see what clothes appealed to us. Erlebacher's carry few items costing less than 50 dollars. I selected a three-quarter-length, scarved coat and matching skirt ($365), and Judy a Thai silk dress and tunic coat. We were both asked to model them to the customers in the salon.

We met again when the afternoon session of work was over and decided how to get home again. We finally went to the Mayflower Hotel and stood waiting for a taxi. We tried to look as though we had just emerged from a smart tea party in the hotel, and joined the mink-coated women in the queue which was being chivvied along by the hall porter. We managed to jump the queue and went home in a cab.

Clambering up the steps of 2319, eagerly anticipating the warmth of the house, we got a shock when, upon opening the front door, a gush of cold air met us. The heater had passed out so we called the Gas Company who promised to send round a man 'sometime'.

'We have probably let ourselves in for at least $6, Judy,' I said, remembering the spoon that got stuck down the waste disposal, and the plumber who took precisely one and a half minutes to get it unstuck and charged that amount.

Upstairs it was below freezing due to the partially open window that we had been unable to shut because it had iced up. Judy raised the venetian blind in order to get to the window, and in the process managed to pull it down. Eventually we did shut the window but the blind hung sadly from one end only.

84

I went downstairs to find something to eat and opened Denise's box of Metrecal wafers.

Out crawled a large cockroach so I shut the box and ate a stick of celery instead. Judy turned on the television set which did not show us anything but flickering lines and specks. So I decided to have a bath to get warm again, and we both ended up doing Tahitian dances a la *Mutiny on the Bounty* which we had seen the night before. One of us banged out a rhythm with a brush on a lacquer tin while the other one squirmed and writhed, hoping to look like Tarita, the girl Marlon Brando chose.

Just as we were getting into bed clad in our new tights and sweaters, the door bell rang and Judy went down to greet the Gas Man. He mended the heater and drew diagrams for Judy (in her muu-muu) showing how to relight the pilot light if it went out again. He charged us nothing, and we put the thermostat needle up to 85 degrees.

Denise was out with her man, The Midget, and I reminded Judy not to put the chain on the door and in so doing lock her out, as had been known to happen before. While the heater roared away below us, periodically giving loud explosive noises which we thought best to ignore, Judy and I tried to go to sleep. This proved difficult. Our negro neighbours were having their usual alcoholic revels, and their dogs, Blackie and Blondie, were joining in.

'. . . Eight degrees outside, barking dogs, drunk neighbours and cold feet – oh, Susie, let's get married!'

Washington D.C.
December 1962

POSTSCRIPT

Yorkshire U.K.
October 22nd 2002

On this day forty years ago President Kennedy spoke
to Congress and the world press on Capitol Hill in
Washington telling them about the dangerous situation
which had developed and was known as the Cuban
Crisis. There were nuclear installations on Cuba and a
Russian warship was steaming ever nearer the island
loaded with dangerous weapons. Krushchev had been
given an ultimatum. It looked as though we were heading for a Third World War.

A palpable fear had taken hold in the city and signs were
put up pointing to the nearest fallout shelter. People had
been urged to buy special food rations. I rang home and
woke my father at 2.0 a.m., their time, and he sleepily
told me that he couldn't really see the point in me

coming back to England immediately since if we were all going up in smoke, it didn't make too much difference if it was in Dorset or in Washington. For me, it took the heat out of the situation and so I laughed and hoped for the best.

SCRAMBLED LIVES

Looking back, I scrambled my own life. I was deaf to my still, small voice within, and would not listen to its persistent warning that the man I had set my heart on was not in love with me. He had admitted as much, adding that, in time, he might learn to love me. He was paralysed with indecision as the affair dragged on and seemed incapable of letting me go, despite his mother's encouragement to do just that. I was used to getting my own way and felt driven by desperation and frustration, and a conviction that I had to move on to embrace a wider and more stimulating world than the one I had previously known. In those days, for girls like me, marriage was the gateway to sex, children and fulfilment.

His family were playing a game, the game the English upper classes instinctively knew so well. It was a comedy of manners steeped in a subtle deceit, hypocrisy and a peculiar brand of cruelty, especially to their children.

Me aged 19

Over time an undertow sucked at their self esteem and often left them floundering in social quicksands. Lonely and eccentric my parents-in-law certainly were and this might go some way to explaining their behaviour. Great wealth muffled cries of inner pain but it allowed a hedonistic lifestyle which delivered nourishment but not always happiness. Like a November fog, failure hung over families such as theirs who had seen better days.

I was a childish twenty-one-year-old when I became engaged to Jake and married him in the Abbey. Now I shudder at the pity of it all, for them as well as for myself.

It was said that the wrong son died in the war. Neil had everything, looks, charm, intelligence and drive – the right kind of drive. Hubert, my father in law and the middle son, was left behind where life so often continued to leave him. But he got into the school where his family had been for so many generations that they were known as 'Founder's Kin' and paid lower fees. Hubert was good at games and his name was painted on the Board of Merit.

Hubert's family was of old county stock, well connected with a whole chapter devoted to them in Hutchen's History of Dorset. Georgiana danced with the Prince Regent at a ball in Dorchester. Her brother was mentioned in *Punch* magazine as having been seen striding down St James's in London with a black servant carrying his parcels. After school and then Cambridge, before the second world war broke out, Hubert decided to try selling fruit and vegetables from a stall in Chelsea. This was considered an unusual and doomed enterprise. So it proved to be.

He soon fell in love with Flavia. Flavia with the double-barrelled name and chin to match. They were married in style in Salisbury Cathedral but her parents decided not to serve champagne at the reception as a mark of their disapproval.

Hubert was left a farm in Dorset together with a dark but attractive old house, Longburton. Maude, his un-married sister, who for years had helped on the farm, was most upset to be turned out of the house to live in a charmless cottage at the bottom of the drive. Brother and sister were subsequently not on speaking terms and the only time in years that Hubert entered her cottage was when he stormed into the kitchen, wrenched open the oven door and removed the Sunday joint of beef which the butcher had delivered to Maude by mistake.

Hubert was reluctant to take advice on how to run the farm and it was not long before he found himself in debt. The couple by then had two sons, Jake, the eldest, and Bertie the easygoing, lucky one. Jake was so lonely and bored in the holidays that he looked forward to going back to school. Bertie attended a couple of crammers which had short, expensive terms and he had tutors in the holidays to get him up to standard for the dreaded entrance exam into Eton. During this time Flavia was kept short of money and petrol. By the end of the fifties it was clear that they had become quite incapable of throwing anything away and the whole place was dying of detritus and damp. Long conversations took place when Hubert rang his son in the City for financial advice which he subsequently ignored. Later it became apparent that he was suffering from premature senility and Flavia was to witness his relentless decline into dementia.

Hubert was at heart an affectionate and demonstrative man. With his outsized hands he used to take tickling too far with his small grandson, frightening him and throwing him high in the air. On occasions he would call his grown son 'Darling'. He liked to hold forth at meals in a fixated way. He disliked ROMAN Catholics intensely and books by Thomas Hardy were banned in the house because he portrayed the Dorset gentry in an unfavourable light. Iain Macleod was a politician not to be mentioned because he had sold off the colonies bit by bit.

Flavia used to make an extremely strong cocktail of gin and lime and 'something else' only darkly hinted at. Picnics were popular in all weathers. Sandwich boxes of tin with rust lodged in the corners and lids which did not quite close were produced, together with thermos flasks coated with tannin and old mugs and beakers in all sizes and colours.

There was dust on everything inside the house. The stone mullion windows let in diffused light and they were framed by thick-stemmed creepers. Inside the flag-stones appeared to sweat damp. The kitchen was large and dark with a huge black range at one end where sickly lambs used to be put in the bottom oven to be resuscitated. Ancient fly-papers dangled from the cross-beams together with pots and pans and colanders. Flavia had to walk a long way from fusty pantry to frowsty scullery to mouldy larder and back to the kitchen. Mrs Batsford helped in the house, her thin hair scraped back into a currant bun. Her husband was the only farm labourer, apart from Hubert's sister, Maude, and two Polish ex-prisoners of war who had, unaccountably, decided to stay on. Hubert stabled some old cars and farm machinery instead of horses – all for a museum one day he told us.

One weekend Cousin Isobel from London came to stay. She was so cold in the night that she got out of bed and switched on the one bar electric fire in her room. Hubert very soon burst in and ripped it out of the socket in the wall. It was five-thirty in the morning and the teats were falling off the cows' udders in the middle of milking because the machine could not cope with the

94

extra load of electricity. The milk was not tuberculosis tested and the water which was pumped from a borehole in the Alderney's field had a strange taste. The sheets and blankets on the beds were damp and the clay hot water bottle did only a localised job. There were brass warming pans hanging in the kitchen but they did not appear to be in use.

Flavia found an outlet for her energies in the occult. She owned quantities of books on the subject. She would seat herself beside a depressed and smoky fire in the oak-panelled morning room and would swing a pendulum over any object still enough to interest her. She announced that my unborn baby would be male. She got that right. Hubert allowed only green logs to be used for slow burning and so Flavia had a mohair rug and a smelly, rather old Pekinese on her knees. She once held her two-year-old grandson up to the window and excitedly pointed out to him a U.F.O. gliding past. As a result he was so frightened he would not sleep alone for several nights.

When telling my mother-in-law Flavia's story it would seem logical to begin in the cradle. There wasn't one. Twenty minutes after Margaret was born in the summer of 1907, with due ceremony at The Hall, another baby girl made a surprising appearance and was hastily placed in the bottom drawer of a chest. This was Flavia.

The twins were subsequently never sent to school but

had governesses to teach them. Flavia rode her donkey to hounds with a Great Dane at her heels. All appeared to be harmonious between the girls until their father died some years later and cut Flavia out of his will. Thereafter they did not speak.

Flavia married at nineteen and lived the early years of her marriage to Hubert in London. Soon after war broke out it became too dangerous for her to remain in Chelsea so she went with her two small boys to seek refuge with her family in the country. There she was allocated half the servants' wing and given only leftover fruit and vegetables from the kitchen garden to eat while Margaret and her children were in the main house getting the best of everything.

For years the ancient fireplaces in the Jacobean house had smoked badly. It was not until the old lady's death that quantities of empty bottles were found neatly stacked up the inside walls of a great many chimneys. Anna, the housekeeper, and her friends had drunk through a pipe of Taylor's Port in the cellar, much of which had been Jake's Christening present. The house was haunted by an ancestor whose portrait hung in the dining room. As a child, Flavia pointed out an armour-clad figure standing at the foot of the four-poster bed she shared with her sister, who could see nothing.

Jake was told from an early age that his mother could see through walls and he thought she might be some sort of witch. He decided, therefore, to put her to the test and prised up a loose floorboard in the lavatory. This was during the war when Bronco lavatory paper was impossible to buy. His grandmother had, however, bought a job lot and it was carefully used so that there was always a supply. He hid an almost new roll under the floorboard and he thought that if his mother could really see through walls she would simply extract it from the hiding place and put it back in its holder. She did not, and so he got another precious roll out of the linen cupboard. He hid that one too – with the same result. When there were three under the floorboard he had a rethink and felt rather perplexed.

In later years, when I knew her, Flavia was a plump, dumpy woman dressed in out-modish clothes, her age indistinct. She had a most piercing look and dark, green-ish eyes. With her suppressed mental energy she had a habit of baring her teeth during normal conversation. She was prone to be negative and was fiercely critical. She alone knew why she felt she had to fight her corner so hard. As Jake's young bride, I found it a daunting task trying to fit in to his family. Unworldly, disapproving and frozen in time, they seemed to me to want to live their lives alone and apart.

I was eighteen when first I stayed at Longburton. When Jake showed me up to my bedroom I noticed that brambles had been carefully twined around the brass bedstead. I pointed this out to him with surprise and he said, "Oh, my mother has been up to her tricks again!" Sleep did not come easily to me that night and nothing was said about it the next day but I did not stay a second night.

There were several members of the family who were dismissed as being 'batty'. They were either shut up on the top floor of large country houses or were in institutions. Direct questions such as 'Could they be epileptic or schizophrenic?' were considered bad form and went unanswered. Hubert's surviving brother was never mentioned because he had ' married beneath him'. Jake's parents communicated with one another in code which sounded to me like a series of grunts.

On my engagement Flavia told me that she wished me to continue to call her by her surname, even after I was married. She was later put out to discover that her son called my parents by their Christian names. She told me after my engagement to Jake was announced in *The Times* and *Telegraph* that "It is a great pity you are not a graduate because I have always felt certain that my son will one day be Prime Minister." Jake had not been to university either since his parents were reluctant to pay the fees.

Hubert and Flavia sent off invitations to Jake's wedding to everyone they could think of, except Hubert's brother and sister, Maude. They did not offer to pay for anything related to the Service in the Abbey or the reception for six hundred guests.

Some time after Hubert's death four years later, Flavia asked her sons to point out to her the pieces of furniture and pictures each of them particularly liked. Jake's choices had blue labels attached to them and his brother's were green. After her death two years later the labels were found to be the wrong way round and it was Jake's chattels which were despatched to Bertie in Spain.

OPINION

Published in The Sunday Times, 28th December 1980.
Woman's Fulfilment is in the Home
Discontent Caused by Minority

Unemployment is said to be affecting women considerably more than men. Surely then, now is the time for subtle reprogramming about the role of women in modern society. For two decades women have been the victims of the materialistic society largely created and fostered by television. They have been subjected to constant plastic pressure, chrome charisma and cellophane seduction. Envy has set in, causing intense dissatisfaction and greed. Values have been overturned; the rug of domesticity has been swept from under their feet.

The modern wife and mother feels guilty to be at home. She is constantly being asked: 'What do you do? Nothing . . . but money must be earned to buy, buy and buy. Buy to replace the temporary and disposable

100

surroundings – the washing machine, the man, the unborn babies. Don't waste time in the kitchen. Buy a packet of soup (even though it is cheaper and more nourishing to make it), frozen veg and tinned fruit, and get out and find a job and your own identity. Unload the children on to a childminder or day nursery, or give them a latch-key to hang around their necks. Don a headscarf and stand in line to anticipate the thrill of that Friday pay packet!'

The fabric of family life is being torn apart by these pressures upon the wife and mother. She is the lynch-pin. A successful marriage is built upon mutual respect, not competition. The roles of the parents are clear cut and utterly natural. The man is the provider and defender, the woman the procreator and teacher. He ceases to be the provider and leader, and the woman assumes his characteristics and becomes dominant, aggressive and, inevitably, disenchanted with her mate.

The role of the woman in the home can be far more demanding than most of the jobs she might undertake outside. Her problems and pressures are constant and varied, her hours endless, but her rewards many, and she may reap the benefits from successful family relationships until the day she dies.

Household tasks can be made challenging. Women are naturally adept at all the crafts, having great artistic resources and nimble fingers. Before the war there was much merit attached to being able to produce home-made bread or jam, and much satisfaction gained in the making. There is again a swing to herbs, weaving and home cooking, but with women being lured out of the nest, where will the time and energy be found to pursue these inherent skills?

I believe a vociferous and militant minority is fostering the discontent among women about equal pay and jobs. A woman wants her man to be in work, not un-employed. Jobs should be first and foremost for him, not her. A woman can and should get fulfilment from having and bringing up children.

Family life will cease to exist as we know it unless the tide is turned. Any children who do manage to get born will be brought up collectively and churned out in adolescence like packages on a conveyor belt. It will be hard to tell the sexes apart, and neither will be satisfied with their lot. But by then it will be too late for them to diagnose their disease, and from habit, they will continue to stuff themselves with drink, drugs and sex as they chase after the money spiral which they believe leads to Paradise.

APLOMB!

It came as a shock when my brother, Pip, told me with conviction that I was adopted. He said he had come to this conclusion because I was the only member of the family who had red hair and freckles. I believed him, weaving fantasies of an eight-year-old about me, the Princess and him, the Pea. I do not remember thinking for one moment that I might have been a foundling.

Five years later Sir Allen Lane, founder of Penguin Books, told me I had 'aplomb' and would 'go far'. He had taken his daughter Claire and me out to lunch on an exeat from school. I thought aplomb must be some sort of scent like my mother's Chanel No. 5 and I was pleased that I might have it. On returning to school I leafed through my *Highroads Dictionary, New & Revised: Reprinted (twice) 1953*, and read the entry,

APLOMB: Coolness and self-possession

Claire thought it must be the way I wore my cloak which was school uniform, because her father had told her that she looked sloppy in hers. Then I looked up

COOL: Slightly cold, not excited

and underneath,

COOLIE: An Indian labourer (Hind.)

None of my friends would describe me as cool since not only am I a Celt, but also a redhead. As for going far, I had been born in war-torn Burma which was six thousand miles away so I imagined I might return there one day. Thomas Hood's poem comes to mind but I remember nothing of the British Military Hospital in Maymyo where I was born, and very little of India where I spent my earliest years.

My mother's family came from the Beerage rather than the Peerage. This thought comforted me when there was talk of revolution because if considered to be 'trade', my fate might have hung in the balance. But,

'When Adam delved and Eve span,
Who was then the gentleman?'

My great-grandfather owned a brewery in North Dorset with over 200 pubs and therefore lived in considerable style. Nevertheless, his son, on inheriting the business, bicycled to work every day despite having two dark-red Wolsley cars in the garage. (Identical models so that nobody would realise he owned two cars.) Was this aplomb, I wondered.

There was a house at Westonbirt, the exclusive boarding school my mother had been sent to by her parents, which was occupied only by girls who had titles. I should like to have been an Hon. and was disappointed when I learned that I could not tack it on to my name at whim. Still, I thought of myself as a 'have' rather than a 'have-not'. Had I started life as a have-not I might have had the strength of character to turn myself into a rather higher achiever.

It is sad that Annigoni did not paint Baroness Thatcher in a cloak like the Queen. She had aplomb. I first met her in December 1975, just before she became leader of the Conservative Party. In those days we lived in a small terrace house in Belgravia with several prominent Members of Parliament as neighbours: Geoffrey Rippon, David Mitchell, Enoch Powell and Christopher Tugendhat. Most mornings one or other of them was to be seen crouching down on the road to check for incendiary devices stuck underneath their cars.*

Alison Ward† rang one day to say that Mrs Thatcher

---

*Airey Neave was soon to be killed by one such bomb when he was leaving the car park under the House of Commons
† Alison Ward, now The Lady Wakeham

would like to see round our house because she had been told it had been 'beautifully done up'. Margaret Thatcher duly arrived at 9 o'clock one morning before I had made the beds, leaving her detective with the chauffeur-driven Jaguar outside. With great charm she asked to be taken around the house and as she went from room to room on several floors, she opened cupboard doors, looked at every nook and cranny, curtain rail and light fitting and announced,

'Very pretty, great attention to detail!'

As she left she said her secretary, Alison, would be in touch with me.

I received a letter the next day, 10th December 1975:

'Mrs Thatcher would love it if you would talk to her about the decorations at their house in Flood Street. Could you possibly meet her at 19 Flood Street at 9.00 a.m. on Wednesday, 17th December? Don't bother to confirm if this is alright.'

I found Margaret Thatcher, then Leader of the Opposition, to be warm, feminine and most likeable, sitting prettily on her chintz sofa fingering a gold bracelet. We looked around her house and discussed how it might be made to feel and look more interesting.

On my next visit we chose paint colours and wallpapers.

The modest house, identical to its neighbours, had hard lines and small rooms with low ceilings. Mrs Thatcher had little doubt about what it was that she wanted – a clean, crisp look, pretty but without frills.

'One should not forget that a house is just a machine for living in,' she said. The rice paper idea for the drawing room was reluctantly discarded as too difficult to hang. I realised with some surprise that she not only intended to paint the walls but also to hang the wallpaper herself.

I was later told by Scotland Yard that they would provide shatterproof net curtains for all the ground floor windows and so I was to concern myself only with normal curtains. The colours decided upon, I was despatched by Mrs Thatcher with a note of authorisation up the road to Peter Jones in Sloane Square with instructions to buy a supply of dark green emulsion for the study walls. At the same time Denis was told to drive out to Kent to pick up some old paint brushes which had been left behind in the flat in Scotney Castle. He had been quietly reading in a chair, and folding his newspaper with a sigh, mumbled something about 'never being able to stand bottle green' – reminding me of Oscar Wilde's deathbed moan:

'Either that wallpaper goes or I do . . .'

He was told crisply to get on with it.

I have no idea how the Press managed to get hold of the story they ran the next day about Mrs Thatcher up a ladder painting her own walls.

A letter from her written on the 11th February 1976 begins:

Dear Susie,
It was particularly kind of you to make a wastepaper basket to match the new dining room curtains. I am thrilled with it and it is quite the smartest in the house!

Margaret Thatcher did not live in the Flood Street house for very long. In May 1979 she won the General Election and went to Buckingham Palace where the Queen asked her to form a new Government. Number Ten Downing Street became her official residence, a rather grander machine for living in.

ELITE IS EXCELLENT

WHY WE CHOSE PRIVATE EDUCATION

Published in The Sunday Times, 26th September, 1982

What is wrong with an educational elite? Anthony Sampson's new book, The Changing Anatomy of Britain, claims that the wrong kind of elite, Wykehamists and Etonians, still fill the corridors of power. How would he qualify quality then? How can the best be better, or does he think the better should not be best?

I have two sons at Winchester College. It costs £10,000 a year out of earned income. We constantly have to justify and defend our decision to give our children such an incredibly expensive education. Our alternative would have been the Pimlico Comprehensive which has an average of forty pupils to a class. At Winchester an average sized class is ten.

Winchester College is an enormously well-endowed

foundation which owns vast acres of land, extensive property, a famous library and many priceless medieval works of art. Its academic excellence attracts the best teachers. The facilities are superb and the setting of the ancient buildings among the Itchen water meadows beneath the downs is hauntingly lovely.

There is an aura of continuity and a quiet serenity about the place which, probably insidiously, permeates the soul so that awareness of the sheer beauty and the spiritual quality of living and working in such an environment must breed and nurture an elite of a sort.

You cannot buy your son into Eton or Winchester unless he passes the preliminary interview and entrance examination. Winchester is unique in that it has always set its own papers for entry, and the thirteen-year-old boy is required to have reached a standard which is equivalent to that of O level. Nepotism no longer operates at all, and the waiting lists for houses are always full. The academic standard required for entry into Winchester has never been so high, and many boys fail to get in to what is one of the smallest, in terms of numbers, of all public schools.

I believe we are giving our sons the best education in the country and that thereafter they will be adequately equipped (not just intellectually) to cope with life. If they are arrogant, it is an intellectual arrogance. They are not the least bit interested in anyone's pedigree. Indeed, they are remarkably idle about bothering to remember names, but do tend to make a mental note of someone's connection with a grouse moor or a villa in Corsica. I do not think they are any more emotionally underdeveloped than their state school educated fellows.

Theirs is a narcissistic attitude to life, questioning, reflecting, drifting, but always receptive, with an unsullied awareness. Their mental and physical energy is infectious. They seem to grasp the sinews of society wherever they find themselves and ride the unexpected with grace and confidence. Their excitement is in living, getting and giving are in its wake.

I can, as their mother, provide a framework of discipline inside which they develop. Respect I consider to be a bonus, and would not demand as an automatic parental right. The generation gap of the modern parent is not particularly discernible, nor, in my opinion, desirable. If a degree of intimacy is expected and does exist between offspring and parent where confidences are exchanged and advice given, then it is the sound relationship of best friend who also happens to be a mother.

'Boring' is a favourite word of theirs, doubly used when describing the life they see their parents committed to. It is unforgivable to be boring, or to be bored by anything. Situations are there to be manipulated to their advantage. They refuse to be bound by convention, and like to emphasise their freedom in the way they dress, and in what they say and how they say it.

Yes, this is a completely new breed of privileged young men. They know that, above all, they cannot afford to be complacent in the present social climate, but that like plants which have had a fertilised beginning in life, given the right conditions they are bound to flourish.

THE NEARLY-MEN

"I would not have dared to speak to my parents like that!" This was the well-worn cry among my friends these holidays. I have just spent several weeks in and out of the company of my two nearly-men, Charles and Rupert, and their teenage friends. I have not been waving, nor have I been drowning, but at times I have been treading water when out of my depth.

They like to emphasise their freedom in the way they dress and in what they say and how they say it. Theirs is a peculiarly contrived accent with closed vowels and an open drawl. Like a Masonic handshake they seem able to identify 'soul mates' in any crowd. I find it hard in a sea of denim and track shoes to spot the give-away Gucci belt or rumpled New & Lingwood shirt. Their girlfriends, many of whom are already on the Pill, flaunt their newly discovered sexuality at parties where these Peacock Butterflies open and close their wings like beautiful secrets.

Edward, a friend of my sons, is to get £500 if he does not smoke before his eighteenth birthday. What he does with the £500 on December 14th next year will be entirely his own affair. His bedroom smells of joss sticks. He told his mother that it heightens awareness. Known to his friends as Runty, he was the only one of them the landlord of the village pub refused to serve because he was clearly under age. The cigarette machine was more accommodating. Strangely, though diminutive in size, his voice had broken which was a distinct disadvantage as far as Public Transport was concerned. He had to practise in a forced falsetto, 'A half fare to Darlington please', for the planned visit north for the Glorious Twelfth. A fair number of pigeons were shot here in the south, and some were surplus to requirements. In order to pay for the cartridges a notice went up in the village shop advertising plucked and drawn pigeon for sale together with a recipe copied from Mrs Beaton's *Game Classics*. This was to try to tempt the 'fish finger brigade' who were told that rook and squirrel pie and pigeon pâté or casserole were great pre-war favourites of country people.

'GLUE SNIFFING KILLS' is a new sign hanging over the counter of the ironmonger in our Oxfordshire market town. Also, 'WE DO NOT SELL GLUE TO ANYONE UNDER 16'. The father of another friend was puzzled when he noticed an entry for forty Bic biro pens on his son's school stationery bill. There seem to be endless possibilities for getting high from sniffing. The cupboard under the kitchen sink must be a potential glue-mine.

'Jonathan is smoking,' his mother confided to me. 'I have found matches in his pocket and cigarette butts in a tin under his bed. I will not condone his smoking by allowing him to do it in front of me,' she went on, flicking open her gold lighter to light the sixth cigarette of the morning. 'It is an expensive, filthy and unhealthy habit which I regret having taken up when I was still at school.'

'Is it wise to encourage them to do this kind of thing behind one's back?' I asked, feeling a pang of foreboding and suspecting, as I did, that nicotine was not always what the boys were smoking.

THROWBACK

Too much about him was a contradiction; his gentleness with outsized hands, spare frame clumsy in its own footsteps, a quick mind, but slow of speech, hair thick as thatch and cobweb lashes framing too blue eyes which pierced without guile. Energy barely contained, his need hung limp with no one to take the slack so that the man-child within came on too loud and too strong in all his dealings. In the watches of the night he was soul silent.

Where the Roman roads cross from Bishopsbourne to Lower Sharpwood a farm of a thousand acres sits high on the chalk downs at one end of Salisbury plain. A rookery in mixed hardwoods, larches and Scots pines is close to the barns and stone houses. Barley barons rule here and in summer the twin-track drone of Massey Fergusons and cars on the A303 drown out the song of larks, curlews and gulls up from the Solent on a southerly.

It was enough, being there, living on the land which his ancestors had owned for hundreds of years. The horizons were as vast as Australia's outback where he had been sent after school to 'find' himself. He returned a decade later ready to help his cousin farm The Ladyacres. The older brother owned the adjoining land – more thousands of acres – a clan, a dynasty, and he was one of them despite his flaxen locks and Aussie lilt to his speech.

'What do you make of him then, Clare?'
'Not a lot . . . Millie likes him though. He's a gentle giant, I'd say.'
'A throwback if you ask me – all that blonde hair and blue eyes!'
'I didn't ask you. You asked me,' she replied.

Clare seemed to him strangely familiar although he had only recently met his cousin's wife and their small daughter. He sensed her presence by instinct, seeming to know where she was and what she was about. Over the weeks he had lived with them it felt as though she fitted in with him, filling ever more spaces in those throbbing days of summer.

It had not started like this: another mouth to feed, more work. Few words were spoken during the lambing month, just staccato sentences requiring short answers or a nod of the head. She had watched him though, soothing the ewes with word and hand and oiling his strong forearm with its white down of hair and gently reaching into the birth canal to straighten a bent leg and ease out a lamb, sometimes having to tear the membrane sack around it to help it breathe. He noticed little things and carefully pointed them out to the child but he made no eye contact with her mother although he was ever aware of her and followed her in his mind and in his heart. These were places where nobody had been before. His cousin thought him sterile like the parched wastes where his only companions had been ranchers and swagmen. Burnt out in the bush . . . Aboe land. But the desert does not die of drought. It sleeps.

When the evenings drew in his cousin went to Southampton twice a week to do a course in land management.

'You'll be all right here with the eunuch, Clare,' he heard
　　him say.
'He is larger than a Collie and you and Millie can see more
　　of your mother.'

And so the short days made way to long nights but he stayed outside, busy with tasks until the dark drove him inside and up to his room over the back stairs where he had a television set and his music and magazines. On the days when they were left alone he would sometimes lie on the floor and play with Millie with his smiling blue eyes and laughing mouth. At Christmas the clan gathered in the brother's house in the valley but he was not among them. He drove away down the long track in the pickup truck and was gone for four days.

When he returned Clare said,
'I missed you.'

In the spring they made love. She wanted him and led him to previously unknown places in his mind and body and for many weeks they lived with brighter colours, louder sounds, sweeter, ever deeper swings of happiness. Then she told him she was pregnant with his child. His cousin would never know because she would have sex with him and care for him again so that he would not suspect anything and all would be well. And all was well . . . for a time.

Then the cold and wet weather rolled in and Clare was with him in the barn cleaning out the feed bins. In the dust of the barley meal she traced a pattern of lines with a stick. He bent over her to look at the spokes of a wheel she had drawn on the flagstones.

'They are ley lines coming out from Stonehenge,' she said. 'The house here is built on one and no cat will stay with us because all that energy makes them feel uneasy.'

Taking a stick from her he drew the pattern of a maze weaving through the lines and told her of the songlines of the Aboriginals and of their dreamtime.

That winter, when Millie was two and a half, his girl baby was born in the Cottage Hospital. His cousin stayed with Clare throughout that night and the following evening they returned home and told him her name was to be Alice.

The first of the unsettling wave of feelings came over him at this time. He felt nauseous with a dread he could only define as fear, a new sensation, fear for himself. Clare seemed to be removed from him – she and his baby all wrapped up in swaddling clothes to shut him out. A very fat girl from the village came daily to help with the housework. He noticed that even her tongue seemed too fat for her mouth, but she was a secret eater and made great play of refusing food and drink or having a 'sparrow's fart' portion as his cousin put it.

Months passed and the summer came and he was left with the girls of an evening when they went out. This was his special time. Clare had said, 'Remember that Alice Springs is our baby's secret name – ALways SPecial – but no one must ever know. If anyone is in danger of guessing the truth you will have to leave here and never see me or her again. Remember too that Alice springs from our love but only you and I can ever know.'

It was then that the white edged wave of anger rolled

in, 'Won't you tell her about me then – as soon as she is able to understand?'

She shook her head and said,
'Never!'

Comment began to surface about how involved he was with the two little girls. People said it was surprising that he was so well able to look after them, baby-sit, cook for them, sort the laundry and make and mend their toys. Clare distanced herself from him more and more and now both she and her husband were free to pursue outside interests because he had become so dependable and indispensable. The fat girl from the village in the valley was told she was no longer needed because the children would be spending all day at school.

She disliked being nudged out and remarked that real men knew their place and instead of trying to become nursemaids and milkmaids they stayed out of the way driving tractors all day. There was no comment about Millie having dark eyes and hair and Alice being so blonde, but the village girl had noticed things and tucked her observations away in the folds of her flesh to be savoured and sorted out later.

Being with the girls was where he found himself again, whole, unsullied, joyful. Their questions opened up shuttered catacombs in his heart from which honey and all things sweet came out in his answers and in their play. He nurtured them as an alpine garden in spring, he groomed them as two thoroughbred fillies, he fed and watered them with the hunger and thirst of half a lifetime, but it was Alice whose blue eyes were the windows to his own soul.

And then they were gone for long periods at a time to boarding school. He joined a sports club and soon became very good at tennis and squash. His eye was keen and he hit hard and accurately. This was control in an uncontrolled time of his life. Playing the game was the discipline he needed and it helped to banish the whisperings of ghosts and goblins.

In was one Whitsun holiday when he had full charge of the girls because the parents were in France that there came a change. Millie had told her mother on her return that they had played bare leapfrog on the lawn one evening. Clare asked if she meant that she and Alice had worn nothing at all and then she said they were too old to have done such a thing. With an unquiet mind she decided to keep her worries to herself but the clouds were gathering.

Millie of the brown eyes was intelligent, sensitive and observant. She loved him with an impulsive extrovert childishness, but as she grew into adolescence she was aware of the flip side of feelings and they hurt her. She saw that it was Alice who ran to him for hugs, books that Alice would like which were chosen to be read, it was Alice who watched the badger cubs playing as darkness fell and who was shown the yellowhammer's nest.

'He gets under the duvet when he reads to us,' she told her mother.
'And what else does he do?
'He feels down the front of our night-dresses to see if our boobs are getting bigger.'

Then it all broke – a terrible storm which washed everything before it in utter devastation. A month later at the village carnival the fat girl's mother said,

'You should watch that cousin of yours with the girls!'

When they got back after the barn dance that evening Millie met her parents in the drive. She was sobbing while trying to talk. Her father went inside and half an hour later a green Volvo came up and two men in uniform entered the house. He was in his room at the back, frozen with shock and foreboding. Alice was in bed and Millie in the sitting room still sobbing in her mother's lap as he was driven away in the green car.

In order to survive the interrogation which followed he altered his mind so that it floated above the concrete, the chemical smell, brutal light and noise in a way that animals behave when herded and only flared nostrils and heaving flanks convey their stress. His shirt was wet with sweat, hand shaking so that writing the statement was a double ordeal. He was offered a cigarette but as he had never smoked one he refused. The police were surprised.

'A great deal about me might surprise you!' he said, sitting awkwardly at the Formica-topped table. After laboriously filling in the form with name, age and address he added,

'Look in the churchyard at Teffont Magna where you will see a large raised tomb covered with a massive single slab of stone. My name is the same as my ancestor's inscribed on it. It says he was laid to rest in the year of Our Lord 1674 and that he was a Gentleman and a Messenger to three Kings of England. I live here where my family have lived and farmed these many hundreds of years and I too consider myself to be a Gentleman in every sense of the word. So I hereby swear that I have never hurt Millie. My life's blood runs through my daughter, Alice, and every hair on her head is precious to me, the air she breathes is also my breath which I would gladly give her.'

He was kept in the police cell all night and all the next day. He said very little. He did not tell them that his ancestor had also been falsely accused, that Cromwell's men had imprisoned him in the Tower of London until the accession of King Charles II to the throne when his lands and position were restored to him.

When leave was granted to close the case against him he disappeared on walkabout to allow the pulse of the earth beneath his feet to heal his wounded spirit.

Meanwhile, the family gathered in a frenzy of dissecting, devouring and trembling with a cold rage and disbelief. His cousins moved from the Ladyacres farm and went to live in another county. Millie's feelings of hurt and betrayal gradually became less painful, but Alice bleeds still. The dreamtime will surely run full circle if they can all wait that long.

TIARA

The ball at Longleat
Less than real, not more
Dreamlike and understated
Rather a tiara than a crown
Cushioned in its hollow of velvet
And all lit up in the night sky
With diamonds and lace
His cradle of memories
Our lodestar
Her face . . .

So they will nail him at Christmas
Like the gathering at Gethsemane
The hurt will be in holly
And the blood in wine
All his shame will be a shroud
And his anguish will be mine.

FIRST PERSON

Published in *The Times*
Friday, March 4th, 1983

Note: All that is described here took place between my two marriages.

Living with an alcoholic is living with insanity where uncertainty prevails. It is impossible to make plans. Anticipation is entirely to do with whether you will find yourself in the company of Jekyll or Hyde, not where or when something will happen. The person closest to the drinker is treading quicksands, desperately trying not to lose sight of normality. I did not feel strong enough to organise my day until noon, after he had finally gone to his office, but then I would start to dread the evening, wondering how I would be able to divert or arrest his grim compulsion.

He drank vodka in the office. It is not easy to detect on

the breath. Sometimes he would ring late in the evening asking me to collect him from work because he had either forgotten where he had parked his car, or knew he was incapable of driving. Usually he rang to say he would be back at a certain hour which I came to know was as uncertain as the weather. He sometimes disappeared for twenty-four hours or more. I used to drive around the pubs I knew he frequented looking for his car, and when I found him he would first of all turn to me with hatred in his eyes, instantly changing to a charming welcome with excuses.

I would come across him sneaking drinks straight from the bottle. He bought half bottles of whisky which fitted in his coat pockets. He would insist on driving himself everywhere, with me following in my car, because his car afforded many a hiding place, and before any social or business engagement he would prime himself with alcohol at the last minute. He drank moderately in company, except when among his heavy drinking friends. What one actually saw him drink was the tip of the iceberg.

He had many brushes with the police while driving, but only once failed to manipulate the court with expensive counsel. On that occasion he lost his U.K. driving licence, so he went to Dublin and got a Republic of Ireland licence. When stopped by police he could reel off his car or telephone number, even though I knew he could not walk without staggering and would take many minutes to fit a key to the lock on his front door.

He was a compulsive liar, and the lies coloured all areas of his life, past and present. He would even lie about how many potatoes he had eaten for lunch. He constantly misconstrued and distorted event and conversations. Met with silence, he would become aggressive and go on to bait and provoke me into saying something – anything to relieve his pent-up agony of mind.

The verbal abuse would usually turn to physical violence, but sometimes he became violent with no warning, almost as though he had suffered a brainstorm. When sober he especially liked my long hair, and when drunk he used to grab hold of it and pull or throw me to the floor where he would kick and punch me. He used to say at such times that he wanted to kill me. I hid my handbag in the washing machine because he had a key fetish and used to try to take them from me to prevent me driving off in the car or re-entering the house if I ran away.

In the morning his remorse was sometimes painful to behold. His memory of events was patchy, but confronted with evidence of his violence the night before (bruises, broken furniture, drink on the carpet or wallpaper), he would be pathetic in his subjugation and humiliation. That he was terribly sick was all too apparent to me, and I was therefore able to be compassionate and forgiving, but my love for him gradually gave way to pity laced with fear. He would ask for love and understanding and for help. His childlike dependency was appealing. With his defences down we could talk about his drink problem, and on a few occasions I got him to go to a meeting of Alcoholics Anonymous and he read their literature. His attempts to stop or cut down his drinking never lasted. As he regained his confidence he would say, 'I can't be an alcoholic. I don't have gin for breakfast.'

He had his last slug of brandy or whisky usually at midnight, plus valium and sleeping pills. In the morning, shaky, sweaty and feeling sick he would light the first of the day's sixty or so cigarettes.

His own doctor was of course not told the truth, and so seemingly entered into a conspiracy in which I was the neurotic and very difficult to live with, and therefore it was me, not him who was sick. He told our friends the same story, and most of them believed him.

He now began to suffer bouts of severe palpitations of the heart. Tests showed a normal heart whose function was interfered with by the excessive alcohol in the blood and chain smoking.

When he became psychotic, I would creep into the bathroom and lock myself in there, sleeping among the bath towels.

He was committing a slow suicide, dying of a sort of

cancer of the soul. Meanwhile, battered and bruised emotionally and physically, I at last sought help. Through my closest girlfriend, who guessed most of what I could not tell her, I was given immediate help by Al-Anon, the 'other side' of Alcoholics Anonymous.

Gradually I was made to realise the alcoholic must want to love life more than wanting to drink himself to a certain death, and that I could not choose for him.

BREAKDOWN

The days uncurl reluctantly
Brown at the edges
My space does not fit me
But seems to grow with alteration
A vapid habit, loose-lived, gaping
Its plainsong finds me wanting . . .
For I have been where the sun can't go
Where floors sweat damp and worms are white
My breath is dank as moorland moss
The cold is as warm as the dark is light
The windows are of mirrored glass
My face their guest of ghostliness
My thoughts are hung on hooks of bone
Martyrs to my loneliness.

SLIDING

There are more than two thousand attempted suicides in this country each week – two thousand people gambling with the ultimate weapon; their own lives.

A bottle of pills bought over the counter is cheap and easily administered. A massive overdose of Aspirin or Dispirin requires an immediate stomach pump to save life, but other drugs such as Paracetamol necessitate the prompt injection of an antidote as well to arrest permanent and fatal liver damage. It is therefore vital that the drug, or combination of drugs, be identified at once. A large intake of alcohol combined with Valium, Librium, Mogadon or one of the other commonly prescribed sleeping pills is frequently used to induce a comatose state.

The para-suicide is often young, and suffers from feelings of rejection and acute loneliness. It is alarmingly easy to disturb the balance of mind to a state where judgement is impaired and swollen and painful emotions throb like varicose veins in the brain. A drug-induced change of mood is deliberate at the outset. Once in the grip of it there is a strong reluctance to surface only to be confronted again with the problems involved with lurching from unhappy night into day and back again.

In the London area the Samaritans receive over half a million telephone calls each year. On average they receive two hundred calls a night. Hospital admissions probably account for only half the number of people who have attempted to take their own lives. Some 25% are re-admitted to hospital with self-poisoning within a short period of time. They are by no means all in need of psychiatric help. They are the victims of impulse born of a deep despair and in many cases need tea-and-sympathy with a friend rather than half an hour with a social worker on Tuesday afternoons.

*   *   *

I threw the empty bottle of pills over the garden wall into an apple tree. Afterwards I was just able to tell my mother over the telephone what I had done, that I loved her, but I could not remember what it was that I had taken. Within twenty minutes I had lapsed into semi-consciousness. The drive to the hospital in an ambulance took another forty minutes. The nursing staff in the Emergency Ward dressed me in a shroud-like garment from which my thin white feet stuck out forlornly on the stretcher trolley and I heard them say 'What lovely scarlet toenails!' The stomach pump, a yellow plastic tube as round as a one penny piece was forced down my throat. It did not go in easily and hurt dreadfully. I was soon very sick, and heartsick too – sick to the soles of my feet.

'It is wine not blood,' they said. 'She must have drunk some red wine at lunch.'

Once in the Intensive Care Unit I had a wire attached from the vein in my wrist to the cardiograph machine positioned above my head. There was an aura of sterile silence, and then more blood tests and yet more pills.

'You are young and beautiful . . . why did you want to die? they asked gently.

'And you are wearing a wedding ring – have you any children?'

I told them my children were away at boarding school and that I was divorced. I added that I thought they would be better off without me and that their father and I shared the holidays, which meant I had them with me for only six weeks out of the year.

From the beginning of our relationship my husband admitted that he was not in love with me. Fourteen years later, the fault-line upon which our marriage had been built led to its break-up and we got divorced. Paying the school fees for our two sons meant that there was little left for my financial settlement. Some months later

I found myself living in a house in Oxfordshire, half of which was in my name, the other half owned by the man I had hoped to marry. I have described the severe problems I discovered he had in the article I wrote on living with an alcoholic. I suffered terrible abuse for over two years, which resulted in my breakdown. During that time I received no medical help and, by then, living on my own, with my two sons away at boarding school, I slipped into a dangerous, secret depressive state. I was consumed with guilt and remorse, fearful that the boys' father would find out what I was going through and not allow them to be with me. Never before had I had such feelings of rejection and isolation. I was not able to recognise and therefore deal with my illness and so its hold on me became ever deeper. Nobody knew what was going on.

The little white pills were a desperate cry for help – that, or a selfish last act – the Russian roulette of a para-suicide.

THE RECKONING

What an old woman of a day!
Grey cloaked and muffled
With a million stick limbed crucifixes
For ornaments, perches for crows;
Where is the flamingo sky, the green snow
And the white light we knew?

Love me, love the upside down
And the inside out of me,
The near and far, the high and low of me,
The joy and woe of me.
Without you, I tried to die
But there are many deaths in life –
Like rooms leading into one another
Connected by double doors
Which swing shut behind you:
Once inside each one seems beautiful
And final in its way

Although you know there is another
Leading out of the one you are in
And that you must go on . . .

But then you are back in the
Grey day outside
And all the wealth is within the room
Of your own soul
And without you are a beggar
And in the gutter of your days.

THREAT

'See you our little mill
That clacks so busily by the brook?
She has ground her corn and paid her tax
Ever since the Domesday Book.'

Kipling's lines tumble with my thoughts over our mill, loved and painted by John Constable, which in recent years has been threatened by modern technology: British Telecom wanted to build five 120 foot high steel dish aerials on the Shreen water meadows at Benjafield's farm near Gillingham in Dorset.

A mill on the Shreen Water in the Vale of Blackmore is mentioned in the Domesday Book and ever since its stones have been grinding corn. The grain from the vast uplands of Salisbury Plain to the east is milled and turned into barley meal, sow and weaner and horse and pony nuts, layers mash and cowcake to feed the stock in the fertile Blackmore Vale. The Shreen is a tributary of the river Stour and rises above the watercress beds in Mere. It joins the Stour four miles downstream at Gillingham near the meeting place of the three counties of Dorset, Wiltshire and Somerset. The Stour rises nearby at the head of the beautiful lakeside gardens at Stourhead.

In 1600 the mill was owned by Richard Perne who died in 1636. It remained in his family for many generations. Richard's daughter, Rachel, married Edward Rawson and they emigrated to Newburyport in the new colony of Massachusetts where in 1650 Edward became Secretary of the colony. He owned 6,000 acres of land at that time and among his descendants was William Howard Taft, President of the United States of America from 1909 to 1917. Paul Mellon has taken back to America one of Constable's oil paintings of Rachel's home, Perne's Mill, or Parham's Mill as the artist knew it.

In 1773 my great-great-grandfather, George Blandford Matthews, who owned a brewery and over two hundred pubs, lived at The Old House in Milton-on-Stour. On his marriage to Charlotte Parham of Norrington near Salisbury, he acquired as part of her dowry a mill on the Shreen. He later built the church at Milton whose graceful spire would have been dwarfed by the satellite station on its doorstep. The mill house is built astride the river and the water lever is controlled by the use of sluice gates and hatches above the millpond.

Matthew Parham was a friend of John Fisher's, who in 1824 was vicar of Gillingham and later Archdeacon of Salisbury Cathedral. John Constable came frequently to stay with Fisher, and he spent many days painting 'the charming undershot watermill near Gillingham'. In 1825 Fisher wrote to Constable: 'The news is that Mat Parham's mill is burnt to the ground and exists only on your canvas.' Constable replied saying: 'I am vexed at the fate of the poor old mill. There will soon be an end to the picturesque in the kingdom.' *

In fact, the horseshoe of grey stone buildings erected in 1830 are imposing and pleasing. The view that Constable painted from the millpond across the water meadows to Mere church with the Wiltshire downs beyond has, as I write, not altered. The area abounds in wild life: snipe, mallard, teal, kingfishers and otters, and with plants such as kingcups and irises, comfrey and cowslips.

The mill has been in our family for two hundred years. Today it manufactures more than 20,000 tons of animal foodstuffs annually. British Telecom did not want to demolish the mill, but had they got their way, the mist might have been seen to cling shroud-like to the water. The church bells would have sounded an echoing death

---

Constable's Correspondence, R.B. Beckett, Suffolk Record Society 1985.

knell inside huge steel saucers and, should we have failed to open the hatches when the river was in spate, Mere might once again have become a lake.

INCEST

They met, this father and daughter, when the war was over after a five-year separation. He was as handsome as any sea captain of her fantasies and she kissed him and clung to him when they greeted one another on the ship which had brought her home from Canada. She was ten, lithe and lanky with huge eyes set deep in a lovely face. She seemed to him to be dressed in every colour of his past and present, and to hold out to his tired spirit every future hope. Meanwhile, her older sister stood by, wary and reserved, and her mother took a step back, silent and suddenly shy.

The family, reunited, moved to the country where her father became a church-warden and involved himself in local affairs. The two girls were sent to a country boarding school, but she had to spend some time at home that first term with suspected tuberculosis.

Her father said he wished to give her history lessons

and they therefore spent several hours each day alone together in her attic bedroom. They had an immediate rapport and were demonstrative in their affection. However, his kisses turned into a slow seduction as he began to fondle her tiny breasts and explore her genitals. Clitoral stimulation followed as he was able to bring her to orgasm and himself as well, although he was not able to penetrate her as she was then too small. At first she was startled and then excited, responsive and eager. Whenever he was unable to come up to her room she masturbated as he had taught her to.

Once more at school, she asked her two best friends if their fathers ever did such things to them. She wondered if that was how fathers taught their daughters the facts of life. She was shocked and disturbed when they were incredulous and horrified, and obviously did not under-stand what she was trying to tell them. Not one of them had heard or even read the words homosexual, lesbian or incest.

Their intimacy continued in the holidays: some-times she went to his room for a 'secret talk' when her mother was out. He told her she was beautiful, that her skin was soft, that he knew her secret places and so only for him would she be able to come alive. He told her that he no longer had sex with her mother and that he therefore needed her and she belonged to him, but she must remember never to tell her mother about the time they spent together as she would not understand, and her jealousy and bitterness, if she ever found out, would make life impossible for them. Other people said it was touching to see such a bond between father and daughter. When she was thirteen she began to menstruate. Soon afterwards she realised that what they were doing together was sinful. She tried not to want or need it. She wanted the father figure of her books who could play an anchor role in her life. She began to feel different and dirty. The knowledge that her friends at school were deeply shocked worried her and she resolved to tell her mother, but she feared rejection from both parents if she aroused the anger of either one. The conspiracy she therefore entered into against her mother increased her sense of guilt and shame. Her inner conflict and stress built up over the months and she developed asthma. Her parents took her for a holiday to Switzerland. After dinner in the hotel she refused to dance with her father, fearful that their obvious intimacy would be apparent for all to see. Her mother was vexed with her for being unkind and forced her to dance with him.

It began to be noticed that her confidence was breaking down. There was a lacklustre about her which was unusual. Her personality was being eroded by feelings of self-hatred. She was attractive to men, but since she was unable to love herself, she could not accept that anyone worthy of her respect could ever love her. She was convinced that someone so perverted and wicked could only attract more wickedness.

When she was eighteen she went to her father's bedroom when they were alone in the house. As usual he came to her and kissed her eagerly, but this time she repulsed him and told him that she was never again going to let him have sex with her. He fought her then, pinning her down on the bed, and opening her legs forced his way in.

From then on she rejected him and there developed a discernible barrier between them which was remarked upon by the family. He, fearful now of her indiscretion, went out of his way to avoid and thwart her.

In her early twenties she attracted men not only by her physical appearance, but also because they sensed she was sexually active and responsive. She became known as a 'cock-teaser', unwilling to let them go all the way but encouraging advances. At a party she heard her friends talking about a girl having had sex with her own father. 'Most incestuous relationships result in frigidity or nymphomania', someone remarked, and another added, 'Or insanity'.

Even though sexual relations had now ceased with her father, she could not rid herself of self-loathing. She considered suicide, she considered consulting a psychiatrist but knew of none. She drifted into relationships and jobs with the emotional numbness of a sleep-walker. Unable to bear the feelings of isolation any longer she confided in her sister. She told her the story from the time when she was twelve. Her sister's reaction was disconcerting: 'Silly old Daddy', she said, 'I should forget all about it if I were you!'

When she was twenty-five she became engaged to an attractive young man. Before the wedding she told him about her relationship with her father. She got the reaction she wanted – he was appalled and wanted to call off their wedding. Had he condoned her actions she would have felt let down. Soon after they were married she heard her parents had separated and that her father had gone to live abroad.

To begin with her marriage worked well enough, but several years later she heard her father had returned to England and was sick and lonely. Her husband had from the start forbidden her to ever mention his name. Her father wanted to see her again. She consistently refused to communicate with him and he died without there having been a reconciliation between them. His death upset her, and she felt fragmented with the old feelings of inadequacy and guilt. Her husband grew cold and distant, impatient with her introspection and depression, and their marriage deteriorated.

She has since sought professional help and has now come to realise for the first time that all these years she had lived in the shadow of her father's problems, not her own, and that she was the victim, not the perpetrator of the tragic perversion known as incest. A month ago she went to the country churchyard where he is buried and laid red roses upon his grave.

Published in *Harpers & Queen.*
August 1984

CONQUERING CANCER

Her life is threatened by a secondary cancer and so her hold on it is tighter than ever before.

These are precious days when nothing is trivial or of little consequence, and all living things seem to shine with a special dignity. The stress in her life, which she has absorbed, sponge like, for nearly thirty years allowing it to fester within, is only now seeping to the surface, exposing raw nerve ends which have for so long been under layers of self-denial and control.

Three years after her mastectomy she discovered a lump in her thorax. The biopsy showed malignant cancer cells. Radiotherapy and drug treatment followed with their distressing side-effects of weakness, lethargy, depression, nausea, insomnia and loss of hair. She afterwards discovered and benefited from the Bristol Cancer Help Centre where she learnt to harness the power of spiritual, psychological and dietary disciplines to help the medical programme.

She believes she can and will recover and that she is able to influence the course of her disease. Her strength lies in her own mind where it can be tapped and utilised at will. 'Know thyself' has replaced 'Forget thyself' as her creed. The daughter of a vicar, and devoted wife and mother of four children, she has long known the emotional ease of a selfless existence, living vicariously through her family.

She has learnt to identify a cancer-prone personality – one who seems unable to channel energy, but in some way blocks it. Anger, resentment, bitterness, grief, envy, fear and despair – all are taken in but rarely expressed. She has learnt to accept and to love herself.

She shares her increased knowledge about living with the disease with her husband and children so that they can, with a deeper understanding, support, help and counsel her. Telling her friends that she is once again ill with cancer proves to be repeatedly painful for she always feels their shock, sadness and fear.

Her Christian faith sustains her. She has books of prayers which she reads and rereads, the familiar words turning anguish into hope.

The intensity of each moment is keenly felt now, and all the compressed yesterdays act like ballast for the uncertain tomorrows. She never asks the question, 'Why me?'

She sees her disease as a symptom and as a challenge,

causing the dead layers of her life to flake away revealing a new found spiritual richness which she feels will transcend whatever is to come, even death.

Published in *Harpers & Queen*, May 1985.

LESS IS MORE

Too precious to be talked about
In platitudes or clichés,
Tawdry clothing for a scarecrow;
We need none
But meet over miles in hallowed cloisters
Damp with song.
Too rare to squander or
Spread about heedlessly
Like grain on poor soil;
Ours is a silver spoon,
Its riches bring us a beggar's heaven
Under a harvest moon.

SNOWTIME IN THE
EIGHTIES

Skiing is a great leveller, at least during any journey up rather than down the mountain. Queuing, which can take up to an hour at a popular lift in the high season, sometimes brings out the worst national characteristics. Most men fall into two categories: those who don't know how to queue, and those who won't queue. The Latin races are in this last group, possibly because they feel it reflects badly upon their manhood. The English/ German entente cordiale is sometimes strained when skis are trodden upon, elbows shoved, or sticks become entwined.

Skiing is as dangerous as you make it. There is a highway code for the mountains. It is foolish to ski alone, in bad visibility, in inadequate clothing, with sub-standard equipment or a poor knowledge of mountain safety and route signs. It is foolish to ski plugged into a Walkman, or to ski too fast.

In the event of a serious accident, lift failure or

avalanche, immediate efforts are made to prevent it being reported in the press, for the ensuing publicity would deter future skiers from coming to the resort. The web of lifts strewn all over the Alps is vast and impressive. There are bubbles, single, double and triple chairs, funicular railways, T-bars, and button lifts, and the ultimate in peak hopping, the cable car into which skiers are packed as in a subway rush-hour. It is often thought that one of the most erotic jobs in the world must be to be paid to stand all day carefully placing a button or T-bar under a hundred bottoms an hour!

The Austrians are graceful and abandoned on skis, legs and feet glued together with much leaning of the body, reminding me of a wind surfer on a bumpy sea. The blonde, blue-eyed Nordic race disport themselves on and off the slopes with an irritating confidence. They are natural exhibitionists, beating the hell out of the moguls and their knees. Many Germans ski to eat and drink, and are to be avoided after lunch. Their style is somewhat aggressive. The Americans tend to be noisy skiers with much thudding and scraping of the piste, and raucous cries of 'Come on you guys', often addressed to a frightened looking group of over made-up matrons from Connecticut. The French seem always to be talking to one another in their exquisite language and manage to look French whatever it is that they are doing. The Australians appear to be bathed in an aura of self-satisfaction at having felt the call of the Alpine snow so keenly that they have journeyed more than half of the earth's surface to answer it.

Ski-bums are of all nationalities, and seem to be rather desperate people who have to keep reassuring themselves that they are loving every minute of their life outside a life to justify their egocentric existence. Skiing is, after all, no character-forming team effort on the whole, but a highly personal and expensive exercise of mind and body. They live as cheaply as possible for as long as possible, chasing the powder when they can.

Ski-bums may be identified by their appearance. They are male, well under thirty, and have a contrived, casual scruffiness about them. Although their skis and boots are usually of the best, their jeans are worn and their anoraks have seen better days. They may wear a silk opera scarf if they are British, and they usually carry backpacks. I imagined these to be filled with avalanche survival kits, flasks of brandy, an assortment of goggles and sun glasses as golfers have clubs, sandwiches and woolly hats. In fact, upon closer inspection, they look sadly empty, like feather-light suitcases often carried in films. Should circumstances force ski-bums to find a job, it is really an admission of defeat because their philosophy is to be as free as air, time and money no object. Some of them become surf-bums in the summer months, living on ice creams and pizzas and sleeping in their cars on the beach. One Swede I met went home to Stockholm in order to draw the dole and returned after a night away to take up where he had left off in the Alps.

One of the best days of my life was skiing alone with my eldest son, Charlie, in the Arlberg, starting from St Anton and then over the mountains to Lech and on to Zurs. Charlie skis fast and silently, his movements like those of a dancer, always fluid and graceful, seemingly in total harmony with his environment. He was a joy to watch.

High altitude is said to affect the emotions and so there is a special intensity about an Alpine agony and ecstasy, but it is that particular kind of high which lingers and makes one feel so good.

THE EMPTY QUARTER

When George Shultz, American Secretary for Foreign Affairs, met Jacqueline O'Brien, the Australian wife of racehorse trainer Vincent O'Brien, they discussed remote areas of the world they had visited and which, in terms of beauty, they considered to be the most haunting. George Shultz said that for him it was that area of the Arabian desert known as the Rub al Khali, or Empty Quarter. Three months later, Jacqueline and I went there as guests of Sheikh Mohammed bin Rashid al Maktoum of Dubai. I kept a log of my thoughts and the events of those moving and memorable few days.

It is the holy month of Ramadan but the four Bedouin, all of them that peculiarly Arab combination of close friend and servant to their Sheikh, break their fast to accompany us on our journey into the desert. They are immaculately robed, and also, as I was to learn later, well armed. Anita, a beautiful Iranian who speaks excellent

English, comes with us in the new air-conditioned Toyota Land Cruiser which is driven by Saeed Manana. Sheikh Mohammed's vet, an Englishman called Dick Collins, drives a Mercedes G Wagon with Ahmed and Abdullah. Mubarak is in a GMC truck with water and provisions, and the two Indian cooks are in a Toyota truck packed with drums of petrol and spare tyres.

We set off in the lead and head south on the road to Al Ain. We cruise at 100 mph, but after a while we notice that none of the others are following. We wait for an hour at the side of the road. Saeed assures us they will come – 'Inshallah'. They do – there had been a puncture. We carry on at speed with the Hajir Mountains of Oman on our left and we enter the state of Abu Dhabi. I see Friesian cows in a milking shed. We stop in Al Ain at a well-stocked supermarket run by Pakistanis with merchandise from every corner of the globe. The Bedouins buy sacks of rice and boxes of Kleenex tissues. Meanwhile, the cooks have called in at the Souk and picked out four goats which are now bleating loudly, squeezed somehow in between the oil drums. I am impressed by the town with its verges of hibiscus, cannas, oleanders, bougainvillea and palms. Sprinklers are everywhere and their efforts to cultivate are rewarded. The outskirts are savannah-like and remind me of parts of India where I spent some of my childhood.

The road eventually runs out altogether and we are on

a rough track. We stop under 'the last tree' and drink tea sweetened with condensed milk and Arabic coffee spiced with cardamon. I notice a packet of cigarettes tucked into the breast pocket of Ahmed's kandora. The truck gets stuck in the soft sand and the GMC has to pull it clear. I come out with some encouraging words in Hindustani and they all fall about laughing. It is now very hot, but a strong wind keeps the heat dry and I feel no sweat. There is no moisture even above my lips. I try not to look at the goats.

We travel on at great speed. The Land Cruiser is comfortable and the air conditioning efficient. Saeed puts on a tape of Bedu music. The wind is whipping sand off the tops of the undulating dunes, and drifts are forming on the road. There are small avalanches sliding down their steep sides. The sand is behaving in the same way as snow. I imagine the vast expanse of gold into white and am transported to a snow-field high up in the Alps. The wind has made patterns like fish scales and ripples of water. The dunes are now mountains. We are still tearing along at a hundred miles an hour. Saeed is singing. The wind is eroding and depositing sand as it has done since time began. We see a pile of stones by the side of the track and place another on top as good luck for travellers.

We arrive at the Abu Dhabi/Oman border post. The guards are prickly and an official letter from Sheikh

Mohammed is produced which immediately placates them. I see a long, long camel train making its way across the desert some distance away and we veer off the track and drive up close. I can't speak for excitement. There is no one in sight until a truck appears on the horizon. My friend, Jacqueline, becomes so carried away with her photography that she manages to stop the train and the camels turn round. We think the approaching Bedu might be angry but the driver of the truck turns out to be a boy on his own of no more than twelve years old. Saeed touches noses with him and I ask if I can taste camel milk. We are surrounded by camels and their young and I fondle them and blow gently on their noses and watch while the Bedu boy milks one teat with a baby camel fastened firmly onto the other. The milk is delicious. The boy has beautiful features and he says 'Thank you very much' and 'Goodbye' in English.

We make camp ten miles from the Saudi Arabian border. Dick tells us he has brought with him scorpion and snake serum. This is not forbidding country, with its green scrub, and many tones of gold and blue sky above, and it has a deceptively friendly feel. The lack of life is what is frightening. No birds or bees, no flowers or trees, hardly an ant, no bugs – but Mubarak did find a large grasshopper which he ate.

Anita and I go for a walk because the goat is about to be slaughtered for the evening meal. The fierce heat has gone out of the sun. I look, apprehensively, for snake trails. We strip naked and pour buckets of water over one another. There is delicious sand here, and across the salt flat is a high escarpment of dunes. How ever did Wilfred Thesiger manage to cross them on foot with his worn out camels?

We sit around a fire and eat bland rice and goat with our fingers. Later we lie on mattresses laid out on a large Persian rug. I watch shooting stars. The air is cool. The men are talking and laughing excitedly for a long time and I miss not having a pillow and wonder vaguely about snakes and their nocturnal habits. Then at last there descends a heavy blanket of utter silence – of a kind I have never before experienced – until Ahmed suddenly sits up and strikes a match to light a fag.

On opening my eyes at 5.00 a.m. after little sleep, I am moved by the beauty all around me and I write:

> Time turns over this land
>> with gentle blade
>>> worried furrows
>>>> laid bare to the glare
>>>>> in the gloom of me
>>>>>> cushions for the mind
>>>>>>> which silence all the screaming
>>>>>>>> as the pain is left behind.

We are now out of contact with Dubai unless we send someone up the tallest dune with a radio telephone. The Bedu are relaxed and happy. They pray unobtrusively and unselfconsciously, turning to face Mecca. Ahmed has given up wearing his kandora and head-dress and has on a loud red shirt. Abdullah cleans his revolver and Mubarak and I swap scraps of French, German and Hindustani. We eat breakfast of rice sticks which I call Arabic porridge and which looks like vermicelli, followed by mangoes. We are surrounded by a mess of litter – the dreadful debris of so-called civilisation. I ask Anita to suggest to Saeed that we should either bury it or take with us. He replies,

'There is no Municipality here to fine us, and when we go we won't be able to see it'.

Litter is strewn over the desert where there is any kind of track. Rusting oil barrels are discarded in some of the remotest places. The American firm, Western Geophysical, is prospecting for oil in this area. They leave behind a sordid trail.

I ask everyone to sign my Thesiger book. The Bedu are fascinated by the photographs, but after lengthy scrutiny Saeed remarks dismissively, 'They are all dead anyway, those people!' A little later he turns to me and says, 'Carlton Tower Hotel VERY OK'. I agree, and ask him if he thinks the Ritz in Paris, where I know he has also stayed several times, is very OK as well. He does.

It is 7.30 a.m. and we are off again, down to only three goats. We tear across the salt flats on which there is a thin layer of white salt crystals which reflect the sun and sparkle like water – a tantalising mirage to thirsty travellers. There are small clumps of emerald green bushes which thrive on salt, but which make a camel even thirstier. Suddenly we all stop dead. The Bedu have spotted a vehicle on top of an escarpment which is the border with Marxist Yemen. Are they police or bandits? Saeed's revolver is to hand.

'They will watch us and track us now, wherever we go,' he remarks.

A whirlwind whips up a spiral of sand and takes off across the plain. In places the sand is baked hard into flaky scales. We reach the point where we must go off the track into unmarked and, to an extent, uncharted territory. We stop and stand just inside Saudi Arabia and photograph each other. I turn round and pretend to run away up the road and they all shout in alarm. To our left is Yemen, behind is Oman and to our right is the vast expanse of the Empty Quarter of Abu Dhabi.

As a child I remember being quite unable to understand the concept of the word 'infinity'. The idea of something going on and on for ever without end filled me with panic. I have the only map which I bought in the museum in Dubai, on which I am able to chart our progress fairly accurately, but from now on we are dependent upon Saeed's instinct, leadership and his uncanny affinity for the environment. The Bedu seem able to harness that uneasy pair of self-discipline and personal freedom. They are steeped in their religion. Its remarkable philosophy colours their entire lives. I wonder at the fundamental difference between their creed from the Koran, 'An eye for an eye, a tooth for a tooth', and our Christian dictum, 'Turn the other cheek'.

Now we are off over the plain leading the convoy and heading north-west. We negotiate foothills, bouncing and sliding through and around the dunes until we gain height, and then we lurch with engine revving, knuckles showing white through my two-handed grip in the back seat. Saeed throws the car upwards, blue sky filling the windscreen and then we poise, teetering on the crest, the sides dropping away sickeningly to unknown heights and depths beyond. These are a truly mountainous range of dunes which Saeed drives through as fast as he can in order not to get caught in quicksands. He seems to know instinctively in which direction to travel and can tell from the smallest change in sand texture, contour and colour how best to proceed.

The Toyota truck with the fuel on board (and the goats) gets stuck and very nearly turns right over which would have been disastrous in more ways than one. The tyres are let down and the Mercedes pulls it clear and then they are re-inflated with an air pump worked off the car's cigarette lighter. We now have a constant thirst which is never slaked, even though we drink all the time.

We are on the summit at last where an incredible landscape unfolds. We see huge plains sprinkled with white salt surrounded by sand mountains which reach all round to the far horizon. We get out of the car and in bare feet we race with Saeed up a sand slope and back down again.

Later on we stop and Dick says the temperature (there is no shade) is around 130 degrees Fahrenheit. We see a desert hare – how can it possibly survive here? Another meal of goat and rice is being prepared. I ask that all the spices we had brought should be used because I was sure the cooks were under the false impression that our English palates could not tolerate their cooking. Ahmed is despatched in the G Wagon to see how high the dunes are ahead. There is concern that we should be forced by the terrain to go too slowly and would have to spend three days crossing the Liwa Sands.

Ahmed is gone for two hours. Is he stuck? The men do not seem concerned and eat with relish and drink quantities of coffee. Saeed strips down and I say, 'Saeed, what are you doing – undressing?' He replies, 'Dressing? No problem!' Ahmed returns having found some Bedu who told him in which direction to go. We continue. The heat is fierce, but there is still a wind which blows hot on the skin. I feel the cruelty in this place lurking beneath its seduction. The air conditioning in the car is not effective while we climb the dunes, but on the flat we feel its benefit. Now the desert is flirtatious again – spreading petticoats of sand with crenellated borders.

Saeed tells us that he has worked for Sheikh Mohammed for twenty-seven years and that he has seven children. He says he has been given everything he owns, and points with pride to his clothes and says he has a fine house in Dubai. I say that I know that he is one of Sheikh Mohammed's most loyal and trusted men. He quietly replies, 'Yes, God has been good to me'.

We are on a plateau of pockmarked craters of a quite different colour and texture to an hour ago. This is real desolation. I feel humble and afraid that there is no end to this oh, so dead land. Saeed is always confident, sensing the way ahead. We find a track which is then obliterated and reappears half an hour later. Oil prospectors have been here and left their litter as well as their markers.

We are very tired. It is evening and still we have not crossed the dunes to the Liwa Oasis. Then suddenly we find ourselves on a dirt track and see a huddle of shacks to the right. Two camels are eating cardboard boxes. A truck approaches and two Bedu boys tell us Liwa is behind us and we have overshot it by about an hour. We are too tired to turn back and decide to camp.

We get through to the Palace in Dubai to say we have successfully crossed the desert from the south.

Another goat is to have its neck slashed and so we disappear behind a dune, hands clasped to our ears and vow not to eat a morsel as it is the one with curls on its head. We wash as before, pouring cans of water over each other. Later, Dick comes to sit on our carpet to talk while the meal is being prepared. He launches into an attack on all things British, including the National Trust. I tell him that as an ex-patriot he clearly feels the need to justify his self-inflicted exile, but his views and opinions of life at home are now out of date. Abdullah finds a large lizard and I shine my torch around and its beam picks out a cream-coloured spider. After eating I decide to sleep in the car because Abdullah has also found the track of a scorpion. I say I am glad the men are keeping their distance as their noise is disturbing. The only remaining goat is lonely and has managed to eat through its tether. I give it a banana and some bread but it makes even more noise and tries to eat a box of Kleenex tissues instead. I long to sleep, but the talk and laughter from the men is louder than ever. Later, by the light of our torch, we see that they are sleeping on the sand and, in order to protect us, they have ringed us round closely.

I sing the Skye Boat Song for Saeed and Ahmed while they make the bread for breakfast. They bake it in the glowing embers of the fire and say they like my singing.

Abdullah then pretends to be John Wayne and swaggers about in his robes with his hands on his hips, saying, 'You Son-of-a-Bitch!' with an American accent. He finds the track of another scorpion near the sleeping bags.

We pack up and head north, but the truck gets stuck. Saeed and Abdullah have target practice from the car while we wait, shooting bullets from their revolvers at Coke tins and water bottles thrown up in the air. 'It is cheating to rest your arm on the sill of the car window,' says Mubarak.

We follow an oil pipeline and travel along a well made up track until we reach the coast road. We bypass the island city of Abu Dhabi and on to Dubai.

September 1985

NOTES:

In appreciation of this article, which was published in Arabic, with illustrations, in the magazine *Al Farah*, Sheikh Mohammed presented me with a gold Rolex watch.

In December 1987 Wilfred Thesiger wrote to me from Tite Street, Chelsea saying how much he had enjoyed 'my remarkable and very interesting journey through the Empty Quarter' and hoped that it would be published in English.

THE EMPTY QUARTER

Time turns over this land with cruel blade
Worried furrows laid bare to the glare
in the gloom of me,
Cushions for the mind
Which silence all the screaming
The pain has left behind.
Stumbling over dunes of memory
Tilted mirrors show star-steps
Worn underfoot from soul searching
Scales drop from deadened eyes;
No bugs, no beetles,
No scorpions or snakes hide here
Under crenellated petticoats
of sand upon sand.
No life, no taste,
No sound, no waste
With shards of fickle silver
As a God's false promise
To clothe this naked land.

RUSSIA

Ten days in Moscow and Leningrad in February, 1986. Ten days where the blandness is all-pervasive and conformity and uniformity are sterilising agents. The remnants of a colourful past, forcibly discarded, are now being carefully, lovingly retrieved from the dustbin of history and held up to the light for re-examination. They are then dusted down, restored and displayed as proof of a glorious and cultured heritage in the many churches, monasteries and palaces. Some of these places have been doubly desecrated during and after the 1918 Revolution and again by Nazi occupation.

A thin atmosphere prevails in town and country alike – a veil of existence which barely conceals the treadmill of survival, the total lack of colour, expression, refinement, style. The vast Russian wastes inspired great creative talent in the past, and all the sensibilities inherent in the Russian character then must be there still. The rows of gaunt, serried, ceaseless flats are unrelieved by any sign of life in the sub zero temperatures. They are even to be found forty or fifty miles outside the cities – seemingly erected on bureaucratic whim and usually built in an unremitting, repeated 'E' shape, the solid concrete blocks extending for a mile or more.

A surprising touch of fantasy inhabits Red Square at night. A mediaeval, cobbled market place with much mellow brick around and a glorious profusion of asymmetrical onion-domes, a peculiarly Russian castellated wall and puppet-like guards goose-stepping to keep warm between the gates into the Kremlin and Lenin's tomb.

Inside the Kremlin there is an air of cold war menace as sleek black limousines whisk Party Officials to and fro, and bunches of frozen tourists are herded from church to statue.

Most of the frescoed and icon-lined churches are now museums, but in the working church the services appear to go on continuously with melancholy plainsong in flickering candlelight. Babushkas, or grandmothers, sit like old crones the world over, fingering their rosaries, their currant eyes black with memories and their mouths taut with disapproval. The need to endorse and identify with events and personalities is fulfilled by the erection of large statues everywhere. Our Intourist bus stops only in designated car parks where boys plead for chewing gum or cigarettes. H.H. Prince George Galitzine, one of our party, was once known as 'Comrade-Prince'. His St Petersburg accent surprised and delighted.

Tourists shop in the hard currency Berioska shops to which entry by Russians is prohibited. The windows are carefully screened so that people outside cannot see the desirable goods within. There is little in the other shops that tourists would want to buy. The Rouble is not a world currency. Inefficiency is everywhere along with a curious lack of wanting to please. Intourist officials plan with military precision what each group should see and do each day. On the afternoon I succumbed to exhaustion and crept to my bedroom after lunch instead of going out again; my telephone rang eight times – once every half hour. It was nobody I knew.

The purpose-built Rossiya Hotel in Moscow had two thousand beds with a vigilant key-lady at her sentry-desk on every landing. No alcohol was sold until after 2 p.m. because of the current concern over alcoholism. In the Moscow Metro, where chandeliers dripped from the ceilings, the only advertisements were huge mosaic pictures of 'Endeavour' or 'Progress' decorating the walls. I saw no one reading a newspaper, even though it was the evening rush hour.

There are now many millions of Muslims living in the Soviet Union. On seeing the seemingly endless queue of people shuffling past Lenin's tomb I asked our Guide if Moslims would be permitted to make their dutiful once-in-a-lifetime pilgrimage to Mecca. I was told, 'Certainly not – only the Priests.'

The Moscow-Leningrad night sleeper express departed at midnight amid platform scenes from Dr Zhivago and Anna Karenina. Inside, at the end of the corridor a charcoal brazier heated water in a samovar for tea. There was no water at all in the lavatories.

On a bus passing through relentlessly flat countryside south of Leningrad, the Guide told us of the crops that were grown in the region, and added that the USSR was self-sufficient. When asked about the recent grain famine she dismissed it by saying that there had unfortunately been some wastage during harvesting and again when one or two lorries overturned in the road.

Rigid guidelines determine thought and deed, and the word 'forbidden' is much used. English graffiti scrawled on a holiday poster in a hotel in Zagorsk cautioned: 'Would the last person to leave Russia please turn out the light.' Its gloom settled on me. When we arrived at Heathrow, I longed, Pope-fashion, to kiss the ground.

GWEN'S WAR

Gwen Beauchamp, my Grandmother's first cousin, wrote an account of her nursing experiences in the Great War:

> I had joined our local Voluntary Aid Division in August 1914 and my father's sister, *Minnie, who was Commandant of the V.A.D. hospital at Mere in Wiltshire, persuaded my parents to let me go to nurse there. So in October 1916 I became a full time V.A.D.

Mere Hospital was in the village school, which was a very modern building in those days – two enormous schoolrooms – one called Kitchener Ward and the other French Ward with four Tuberculosis huts (two occupied at that time) in the playground. Matron told me that another full-time V.A.D. was arriving the next week and

*My Great Grandmother, Minnie Beauchamp White

that she would train us as though we were First Year students in hospital. My opposite number did go on with her training after the war and became a Sister at Barts. and married a doctor.

I shall never forget my first day in the hospital. I was told by Staff Nurse to get a broom, dustpan and brush and sweep Kitchener Ward. Having seen a bottle under every bed I felt I couldn't face it so I went and locked myself away in the loo in the school yard, next door to the broom cupboard. Shortly afterwards there was a banging on the door, 'What are you doing, Nurse? Come out at once, get the broom and sweep the ward.'

Staff Nurse waited until I came out and escorted me back to the ward and watched me to see that I took each bottle out to the sluice before sweeping the floor. By that time the troops were enjoying it and making ribald remarks so that I wished the floor would open and swallow me up with all my brushes and blushes.

One day Matron helped us move a badly wounded patient on to a waterbed; a difficult job as he had a large wound in his right thigh. Having eventually got him reasonably comfortable, Matron started to do his dressing assisted by Sister and a V.A.D., training to be a nurse, who was told to hold a large bowl of swabs in lotion. When Matron removed the old dressing and exposed the wound, the nurse passed out and in doing so poured all the swabs over the wretched patient and his bed. After that it was decided that she was not cut out for nursing.

One day Sister asked me to scrub out a tall cupboard in the ward. I think I got myself wetter than the cupboard and the troops roared with laughter and even the really ill ones joined in to give me advice of one sort or another – some of it very unsuitable. Eventually Sister came in and joined in the laughter, and she showed me the drier way to go about it.

I shall always remember my first day in the Theatre at Mere Hospital. It was a wooden hut in the school playground with a galvanised iron roof. Matron was a very small, extremely capable and terrifying woman. The staff and troops were all frightened of her and I had nicknamed her the 'Mighty Atom'. She was holding a bowl of sterilised instruments in lotion for the surgeon. I can see him now standing there in his braces and shirtsleeves with no mask, no overall, no rubber gloves. Sister from Kitchener Ward was giving the anaesthetic and I was just standing there, ready to do whatever I was told. We were all straight from the wards, possibly washed but certainly not scrubbed-up and dressed in our normal clothes. The patient was a local RNVR (Royal Navy Voluntary Reserve) man on leave with a double inguinal hernia. The operation was in progress when it suddenly started raining heavily. Rain on a galvanised roof is very noisy. There was a flash of lightning and a terrific clap of thunder overhead whereupon Matron became white as a sheet, pushed the bowl of instruments into my hands and rushed out of the Theatre and did not return. I can't remember what happened after that, except that the operation was a success and the patient recovered well so presumably I must have done what was required of me. We found out afterwards that the 'Mighty Atom' was petrified of thunder and lightning – the one phobia over which she felt she had no control.

In 1917 I went home to Norton Hall in Midsomer Norton for Christmas whilst awaiting a posting which I had applied for. It was to the Military Hospital in Bath, not far away. I started work there on January 11th, 1918.

I was on night duty in February – a six-week stint in those days – and when we came on duty Sister told us that Corporal Harvey had died an hour earlier and she wanted Staff Nurse to lay him out. Staff Nurse was in love with Corporal Harvey who had been in Number One Ward for some months with kidney trouble and had died of uraemia. When Sister had gone off duty, Staff, a charming Scot, came to me crying, and said she could not cope with laying him out and would I do it if she told me what to do? So she sat and cried at the foot of the bed and did so. The next day, February 10th, was my 21st birthday and Matron gave me the night off to go home for the party, but I was not feeling much like it.

I was on duty in Number One Medical Ward when we had two cases of pneumonia. One old boy was very ill and a younger man, slightly dim, was much less ill. The old boy's wife was sent for as he was on the danger list. When she eventually turned up everyone gasped with surprise as she was an East End Coster woman with a voice like a hacksaw and feathers in her hat. Directly she arrived she started cursing him for dragging her down from London to see him. We felt sorry for the old boy. She did not stay long and when she had gone he called me over to his bed and said,

'My trouble-and-strife has just told me she's gorn off with another chap and she don't want me no more. She's throwed me kids out and she knows I loves them a hell of a lot and now I ain't got nothing to live for – so don't bother with me no more. I am bloody well going to die.'

I said, 'Nonsense, of course you are not going to die. When you are feeling better you will start thinking what to do for your children.'

Sister called me and when I told her she said, 'Poor old boy'.

Meanwhile, the younger patient had two boiled eggs for lunch. He took them out of the egg cups and threw them across the ward towards the old boy's bed saying to us,

'You'd better give these to your pet – none of you bother about me and I'm as ill as he is'.

He was always making a nuisance of himself and wetting his bed on purpose although he was not incontinent. From that day on the old boy went downhill. It was the only time I saw someone die who had made up their mind to do so.

It was certainly hard work but I loved it. Once or twice I was on duty from 7.30 a.m. until 7.30 p.m. the next evening. On one occasion, when there had been a big battle going on, the convoy arrived very late at night. By the time the men had been blanket bathed, their clothes sent to be 'stoved' and dressings done, there was just time for us to go and have breakfast before we came on the wards again. We were too busy for any off duty time that day, so it was not until 7.30 that evening that we eventually went off.

There were no pre-meds in the time of the 1914 war. One day, when I took a heftyAustralian on the trolley to the theatre, the anaesthetist and I had a dreadful struggle trying to get him under. When we at last succeeded and wheeled him into the theatre, the anaesthetist gave a huge sigh of relief and said to the surgeon,

'Thank God for a strong and capable V.A.D.! But for her you wouldn't have had the patient in here at all.'

One day, when I was doing the rounds with a Doctor, he asked me to take a note of a particular medicine which he needed for a patient to the dispensary. I put my hand into my apron pocket to get out my pencil and scribbling block and produced a pack of cards. Rather embarrassed I put my hand into my other pocket and produced an ashtray! The patient in the next bed had seen what was going on and said,

'Nurse, Private Higgins wants to speak to you'.

So I went to his bed and he produced my block and pencil from under his pillow. When I had been doing his leg dressing earlier he had swapped the things out of my pocket for the cards and ashtray from the top of his locker. I was surprised I had not noticed as our aprons were very tight fitting. I later found out that he had been a pickpocket before joining the Army.

The senior ambulance driver, a friend of mine, came to the ward and asked Sister if she might speak to me. She asked if I knew what had happened to the Canadian Corporal who had been missing from my ward overnight. She went on to tell me that he had tried to commit suicide by jumping into the River Avon. In Court that morning, when asked why he did it, he said 'Because Nurse Beauchamp wouldn't marry me'. I was flabbergasted. I did not know him any better than my other patients. He was young and rather shy. I cannot even remember what his wound was. When one day he asked me if I would go back to Canada with him when the war was over I hadn't the foggiest idea that he was proposing marriage!

I remember doing the rounds in tents one night with a

hurricane lamp and suddenly being aware of an eye staring at me from the top of a bedside locker. It was very startling and we found out the next morning that one of the new intake (RAOC) had a glass eye which he always took out at night but no one had been warned.

The first convoy of mustard gas burns from the front came in. One of the tents had a side ward with very bad burns to Private Parts, as we called genitals then. Sister told me she would show me how to do the first dressing. We had to bind the damaged part with narrow strips of bandage, spread with an ointment, (Eusol I think). Sister and I went behind the screens to the first bed and I removed the patient's pyjama trousers and Sister removed the old dressing. Then she took hold of the damaged part gingerly with a piece of cotton wool, swabbed it and redressed it. After having watched her closely I carried on with the rest of the cases. A nice Australian patient with one arm in a sling was able to help me move the screens and he pushed the dressing trolley for me. We had some Americans at the other side of the ward, one of whom had a minor arm wound. He started crying as soon as I approached with the dressing trolley. This happened every day in spite of caustic comments from the mustard gas cases who were in great pain.

After a week I went behind the screens to do the mustard gas dressing of a RAMC Corporal. On taking off his dressing I said,

'Oh dear, this is terribly swollen today – I had better call Sister to come and look at it.'

He quickly said,

'Don't worry Nurse. It will be all right if you dress it as usual and there will be no need to call Sister'.

It was not until I got married in 1924 that I understood what was happening to him.

On November 11th 1918 I had been on night duty in W. Tents and could not sleep much in the daytime. As it happened that day I was so tired I had gone to bed at 10 a.m. and was still awake at 11 o'clock when all the Church bells started pealing announcing the end of the war. I can remember thinking 'For goodness sake stop those damn bells so that I can get to sleep'.

When we got to the Hospital that night we heard that a large convoy was expected and it started arriving as soon as we got to the wards. The stretcher bearers had been celebrating too much and so were unable to negotiate the duckboards and most of the patients were deposited on their stretchers on the flower beds outside the tents. Every patient had to be stripped and their clothing put into a sack to be disinfected. Each had to have a blanket bath and have his dressing changed. This was a horrible task as most had only the dressings which had been done several days before in the Field Hospital. I remember one dressing which I had to change was for a London Bus driver whose top joints of three fingers had been blown off and were just hanging by a bit of skin. He was operated on the following day and his dressing was the first post- operative one I had to do. I was terrified in case I found the fingers in the same state as previously. Luckily, all went well and he made a good recovery.

On Armistice night no one could recognise Corporal Jones's rendering of the Last Post which he played at the Hospital gates every night at 10 p.m. His performance varied according to how long he had spent in the 'local'. There was a young farm labourer from Devon in Ward One. He was only about 18, having lied about his age to get into the army. The troops used to pull my leg about him and call out,

'Come on Nursie, your little boy won't go to sleep till you've tucked him up!'

The V.A.D. in No. One ward always had to cook the meal for Night Sister, Staff Nurse and herself. I collected the food in a basket on my way to the wards. One night, Night Sister said,

'Nurse, I think you have made a mistake tonight and put sugar on the chops instead of salt and pepper'.

I replied that I was sure I had not done so but next morning everyone was complaining about the same thing. It turned out that the consignment of meat sent down from London by the War Office was horse flesh.

One patient had gas gangrene of the lungs. His bed had to be beside the French windows halfway down the ward because of the unpleasant smell. He always seemed to want something when I appeared and one day he apologised to me and said,

'I'm very sorry I always bother you, but when I want a bottle or something I try to wait until you come along as you are the only one who doesn't avoid me and look as though you are going to be sick because of the horrid smell'.

I remember my last day in the hospital in February 1919. There was a bad epidemic of Spanish flu and gastro-enteritis amongst the staff. We were reduced to one Staff Nurse and me to look after 56 beds. The Assistant Matron came round and asked to speak to Staff Nurse Jones. I got a slate and wrote, "Staff Nurse has gone to the dispensary to collect medicines." The A.M. said, 'What is the matter with you, Nurse?' and I wrote, "I have lost my voice", whereupon she took my pulse and temperature and announced that I had a temperature of 103 and must go off duty at once. I wrote, "Can't leave – only Staff Nurse and me on duty. Everyone else ill".

However, I was sent off to the Sick Room where I was quarantined and given special nursing care until I was sufficiently recovered to be given sick leave. Later, my doctor at home refused to allow me to continue nursing even though I had just signed on for another six months.

When I was fully well again the Commandant of our large Red Cross detachment retired and Countess Waldegrave asked me if I would take it on. So, until I was married four years later I was Commandant of the Red Cross, Somerset 28, at Midsomer Norton.

SISTER ELLIOTT

The only AIDS unit in Britain is at the Middlesex Hospital in London, set up and run by Sister Jacquie Elliott, aged 27. She has seen the disease and its consequences at first-hand.

She talked to me in 1989:

An old head on young shoulders? People might say that, but such wisdom as I have has come through my wonderful patients. They are the most remarkable people, all of them. Don't think they come here to die. Of course, some do, but many get better and go home. Coming here isn't a death sentence. We treat specific diseases – pneumonia or sarcoma or whatever – and the patients get expert counselling advice to come to terms with AIDS, both from us and also from James Pringle House, the clinic for sexually transmitted diseases.

The first AIDS patients were nursed here in the Middlesex in 1982, when the normal precautions for treating contagious diseases were those we use today. In my experience Hepatitis B is more easily transmitted. Of course, I agree that the types and contagious properties of the HIV virus are still not clear. But you can't catch it from sitting on a lavatory seat or sipping from someone else's Coke tin. An infected toothbrush is only a risk if a lot of contaminated blood gets mixed with healthy blood. It is primarily a sexually transmitted disease.

The media hysteria is now counter-productive. People are confused. Some over-react while others are laid back sceptics, which is understandable. The initial Government advertising was mega-dramatic – all those lilies and gravestones and gloomy music! Can you imagine how my patients here felt when they got that on television several times a day?

The leaflets were ambitious, but they didn't reach every household in the land. I didn't get one. But I regard Richard Branson's light-hearted touch with the condom advertisements – the one about the shy young man forcing himself to buy them over the counter – as a more intelligent approach for the man in the street.

HIV is life-threatening, unpredictable and progressive. Especially distressing is the way it too often affects the brain. Demented, prematurely old people are tragic and they will surely present a severe problem to the NHS. Funding is crucial. There will have to be more outpatient facilities offering chemotherapy and all kinds of counselling. Patients will not always need hospital beds, but they will need full time care. There will probably be units like ours in every major city before long, and I have no reason to doubt the World Health Organisation figures on the AIDS epidemic.

I can't bear to think of the leper colony solution we hear of abroad. Why AIDS, when there has been syphilis and cholera and leprosy? We have always had to live with killer diseases. Segregation is moral cowardice. For me, the patient's feelings are paramount. The right to confidentiality is fundamental to caring and test results should only be divulged to the partner or family at the patient's request. I feel doctors who continue to practise knowing they are HIV positive, or even with full-blown AIDS, must decide for themselves.

AIDS symptoms are infinitely varied. The drug AZT is so far proving satisfactory with no apparent side-effects. Worldwide, there is a minor breakthrough every week. With so many people working on it now I am optimistic we shall be able to produce a vaccine. I suppose widespread testing will be compulsory before long. That is probably inevitable and everyone will have to be vaccinated at birth. Could the AIDS virus be insect-borne? There has been talk of this – head and pubic lice and suchlike, but nothing is proven.

I don't wear gloves with patients, but I avoid unnecessary risks. Anyone on any ward would wear gloves to clear up vomit or a soiled bed, wouldn't they? I try not to let my patients feel they are being treated differently from the others. I haven't had a blood test myself, but I could. The virus has been found in tears and in breast milk and is very apparent in semen. But saliva is an unlikely agent of infection except in large quantities. The same goes for menstrual blood in swimming pools or in sexual intercourse. Most of our blood supplies come from this country, but we do get emergency supplies from abroad.

My training means I see only a sick person so I am not tempted to make moral judgements. What would I feel about a patient dying of an AIDS contaminated transfusion in the bed next to a homosexual? That is interesting. I am needed at three levels – the medical, the practical and the emotional. But dwelling on why a patient is here in desperate need of medical care is not my function.

I feel very much protected by my uniform. Whatever anguish and pity I may feel underneath, outwardly I must always be calm and controlled to instil confidence and reassurance.

AIDS has a morbid curiosity for the public and I have had to become a ruthless 'bouncer'. If the publicity I have had has helped the patients, I am pleased. There are twelve beds here in the Unit and I am in overall charge and I also recruit staff. I look first for common sense.

That is important because people who live and sleep AIDS would soon exhaust themselves. Passionate involvement is not really desirable because it is a highly charged atmosphere anyway. What I look for is an almost matter-of-fact attitude masking a deeply ingrained professionalism. Yes, I do have to tell people test results and it is always very hard, very upsetting, but one gets used to it.

The counselling bodies are wonderful, especially the Terence Higgins Trust. Other organisations help in a thoroughly professional way and the Buddies, who befriend an AIDS patient and see him through, are an enormous help.

Hospices? Well, when one of our patients goes to a hospice (I hate that no-hope word), we fill in the accompanying form only as 'suffering from a malignancy', and do not specify. It is nobody's business why a person is terminally ill. At least, that is what I believe. If the patient wants to tell people about his illness, that is up to him.

When the plan to establish the first AIDS unit in the country was mooted I put my name forward. There was a degree of professional jealousy when I got the job and some people thought I was too young and inexperienced. But I knew of the dangers inherent in nursing these patients, and one learns daily about the disease. I see the work as a challenge. Though I am not aware of a sense of destiny, I do have a deep feeling of satisfaction when I feel drained from having worked my shift – when I know I have done my best and managed to make the right decisions and say the right things. I see suffering of course, but I nearly always manage not to take the sadness home. I am not really ambitious and I could not possibly tell you what I would like to be doing ten years from now.

I have never known what it is to be seriously depressed and anyway, I think that I have no right to feel that way. How could I with all this suffering around me? Watching life ebbing away is always a distressing experience, but one which we, as nurses, are very used to. The main thing is to see that the patient is free from pain and surrounded by those who love him. There must be dignity in death.

SAFETY NETS

It helps to have a long-stop, a reserve fuel tank or a safety net in your life. I have been lucky enough to have had all three at various stages.

An air of loss hung about my grandmother. As a child I saw it as a gossamer veil of grief smelling sweetly of violets because she no longer had a husband or an only son. In old age her smile was sad but she had no wish to die because she so wanted to 'know what happens next'. She told me she found it irksome to be relegated to the wings rather than take centre stage where she could influence events. Although physically a strong-looking woman, she was tall with definite features, her emotional frailty made her vulnerable and accessible and, despite a forceful character, she was warm and generous. Because she was utterly sincere in her interest in everyone else ('never think about yourself darling – it will lead to great unhappiness'), people felt compelled to tell her their secrets even though they had reservations about her discretion. She found it difficult to control her emotions – as when taking her daughter back to school at Westonbirt my mother remembers having to admonish her in the car by saying 'Oh do stop crying, Mum!' and her brother, Philip, had to remind her never to kiss him until they were well away from the confines of Marlborough College.

Granny 'lived on her nerves', taking a merry-go-round of pills towards the end of her life. She had quantities on her bedside table and admitted getting confused with her happy pills by day, the sleepy pills at night and saccharine for her early morning tea kept in a tortoise-shell pillbox beside the aspirin for headaches. She found that a good way for getting off to sleep was not to count sheep jumping over a stile, but to go through the names of all her nieces and nephews and then cousins. Her walnut dressing table was white under a hectic dusting of face powder where a dirty puff attached to a square of pink chiffon lay on top of silver-backed brushes. Several fine hairnets floated about like lost clouds and some were stuck to very old lipsticks with no tops to them.

My grandmother cared little for material possessions but it was the privileged attitude of casualness. If she spilt water when topping up the vases of flowers she would say, 'Oh bother, Olive will clear it up!' and then forget to call Olive, Mrs Foot or anyone else. The furniture suffered as a result. She called me her 'Ducking-bird' and seemed always to be there in my life as a long-stop, chewing her lower lip in consternation as I poured out the problems I could not share with my parents, her deep set pale blue eyes watery with compassion as she wrapped me in intelligent concern and wise counsel.

In the years after the war my father owned a succession of cars, all of which came fitted with a reserve fuel tank. This built-in feature was providential as he disliked stopping to fill up and was a compulsive (low) risk taker and therefore good at provoking one of my mother's anxiety states. She had good reason to be fearful that we might be about to run out of petrol in the back of Dorset's beyond in unfriendly weather. I remember this happening, and the knowledge that the reserve tank could be brought into play when the needle on the dial was at empty was a relief. Where exactly the tank was located in the car, one model being a Jaguar, was as mysterious to me as to whether or not it might be half full, half empty or simply non-existent.

One wild night, returning from our boat at moorings on the Beaulieu river, we came to a halt somewhere near Badbury Rings. This was due not to lack of fuel on that occasion, but to a complete failure of the car's lighting system. We had no torch and could see nothing. In total darkness we drove the twenty miles home by memory. My brother and I leaned out of the windows shouting instructions, with my mother crying, 'George, do look out!' every five minutes. It was like standing in the bows of the boat swinging the lead as we entered Newtown Creek on the Isle of Wight.

My father was passionate about the chess of sports – golf, and used to tell me to resist the urge to cut up the turf, to try to be more patient. The bright side of life shone uppermost for him and his banner was 'anything for peace'. He never failed me and was always there with his personal reserve tank when the chips were down and the needle on my dial stood at empty.

My husband is my safety net and if I happen to fall into a briar bush he always manages to get me out. If he dies before I do, I might well become a lost cloud floating somewhere above my grandmother's dressing table.

LORNA'S STORY

I have been where the sun can't go
Where floors sweat damp and worms are white
My breath is dank as moorland moss
The cold is as warm as the dark is light
The windows are of mirrored glass
My face their guest of ghostliness
My thoughts are hung on hooks of bone
Martyrs to my loneliness

Lorna read these words, massaging them, working them as worry beads, sometimes wrapping them round her scarred wrists. Who cared where she had been? How could she have a past or a shadow, an echo or a footprint if she could not find her own soul?

The therapist at the clinic urged her to write her own story and when Lorna was unable to begin she said, 'Just describe your mother and your father in three words . . . three words each and I will write them for you and that will be a start.'

So, as she managed to extract the tufts of teased memory she found she was once more the dark-haired, dark-eyed child of more than thirty years ago when it had all begun.

The birdsong in Norfolk seemed to her to be more strident than elsewhere and their dawn chorus used to wake her in the gentle times of year. More often though she was woken by the grumblings of one hundred year old water pipes coming to life and then she knew her mother, awake on the floor below, was in her bathroom getting ready for the day. She longed for her to come up to the nursery. Could she not go down to her? She never did and nor did her brothers. Nanny Allen ruled their childhood up there on the top floor of The Manor House. She drafted their dreams, and nightmares, chipped and chivvied away at their characters. The damage she did was locked inside those little hearts, stifled, muffled, with the hurt visible in the eyes of each child.

Nanny Allen had a boyfriend. Ken came to the house in the evenings at bath time when the children's parents were in London. In the bathroom there was a wooden laundry box and inside under the cork lid was a rope. Ken used to get it out and tie a lasso and whirl it around his head and let it land on naked shoulders like a rattlesnake. He would laugh and say, 'Giddy-up, heigh ho, I'm a cowboy!' as he pulled it tight. Then he would climb out of his jeans and ask Lorna to stroke his horn and she would have to lie down on the tumble-twist bath mat and be still as a cactus flower. Then he played what he called 'our games' with her and then with the two boys, one at a time, while Nanny Allen sat on the laundry box and watched.

As Lorna wrote, she pushed her hair back from her face and remembered how innocent they had been, having no idea that any of these so called games were wicked. She felt again the pain and the bleeding. She also remembered how all three children frequently sat up in bed in the night and in and out of sleep they banged their heads hard against the wall. It was loud enough to be heard in the room next door but not on the floor below.

Her mother was as brittle as a brandy snap, in-securities barely hidden beneath awkward body language and nails bitten to the quick. Her quick and attractive smile – swooping like a swallow, ducking and diving, said, 'Look at me but don't challenge, don't stay'. Most of her life was lived in the large house beneath the nursery floor. She clattered up and down the polished oak staircase, she busied herself in the kitchen making puddings and pies. She fed her bantams twice daily with mixed corn and leftovers and she watched the serried rows of vegetables flourish in the walled garden and waited with mild excitement for the picking, pickling and freezing to come.

Most days she drove into the village to shop. She did the monthly flower rota in the church, young in years, not young at heart, a heart wrung out on a rack of guilt because the children behind the green baize door on the top floor were being fed and watered by Nanny Allen. She never looked up at the house in case one of the faces was looking down at her.

Friends who came to the house felt the tense atmosphere and worried about the children who were trussed up in emotional straitjackets. One friend heard Nanny Allen warn the children that any toys left out on the floor at bedtime would be thrown away in the dustbin downstairs – and indeed they were. Another friend was so concerned that she wrote a letter to the children's mother describing a regime bordering on cruelty which her own nanny had witnessed on the nursery floor on top of the house. This letter was shown to no one, not even to the children's father and Nanny Allen continued in her job for another two years.

When Toby was eight he was sent away to prep school. Lorna was distraught and cut her wrists with a kitchen knife. She was six years old. When the time came for the other children to go off to boarding school Nanny Allen finally left. But before her departure she and Ken got married with Lorna as their bridesmaid.

199

During the holidays she was sent to stay with them one weekend. She was so frightened by what the couple tried to make her do that she broke an upstairs window and jumped out, cutting herself badly. Lorna's end of term reports said that she lacked concentration, that her work tended to be slapdash. Her mind was all too often focused on her brother and his friends at the boys' school at the other end of the town.

After leaving school Lorna slithered over potholes of misery, grabbing sex and drugs on the way, not really caring where she was going. After several unsatisfactory love affairs she fell for Ben, an upper class vagabond. Despite warnings from her father that he had reservations about the young man, she married him with much pomp and circumstance. Her mother, however, was relieved to have her daughter 'safely married off.'

Lorna very soon discovered that her husband was also wedded to the whisky bottle which he had come to believe was more essential to him than the woman he had married. So Lorna's well-being, except for her cheque book, was of little consequence in his scheme of things. At first, he had affectionately called her 'my completion, my all', but later he complained that he had not been told that he had taken her away from her brother, Toby, and he called her 'soiled goods'.

Lorna began to slide into severe depression. Her voice altered and became low and rasping. She was withdrawn and unable to engage with her children. The drink and drugs only plunged her deeper into despair. Her feelings of failure in all the roles expected of her obscured hope and blunted judgement.

An argument which began in front of the three small children ended with a razor blade and blood in her bath. That was the start of a two-year battle to save her. Lorna had become a compulsive and persistent self-mutilator. She tried to hang herself with a rope from a beam, she took pills and poison where she could find them and cut herself with any sharp instrument she could lay her hands on, once, even unscrewing the blade from a pencil sharpener. Ben had two bolts fixed, top and bottom, on the outside of her bedroom door. But by then he was trying to lock more than his sick wife inside her room. He and close members of her family, each with a different motive, had entered into a conspiracy to keep her father from learning the truth and thereby being able to help her, even allowing the finger of suspicion over sexual and emotional abuse in her childhood to be pointed at him. Ben had been addicted to cocaine for several years. He had much to hide, but in this situation he was legally, as Lorna's husband, her next of kin and her future lay in his uncertain hands.

Ben had his wife admitted to a hospital in Birmingham where she remained for nine months. He gave his permission for fourteen sessions of electro-convulsive therapy to be administered without a second opinion. By this time her father had found out most of the shocking story of his daughter's descent into a depressive illness, but a web of deceit and denial was spun by the family to block his efforts to have her treated by the best doctors available. He was told that Lorna did not want to see him. It was in Ben's interest to prevent his wife's father from being involved. Lorna had an uncomfortable relationship with her mother who, so often it seemed, could not cope with reality. Lorna's brothers and uncles were not inclined to question her husband's agenda. Their neglect of their duty, as trustees in her uncles' case, could have been life-threatening.

Lorna was sent to a clinic in Arizona for further treatment. The doctors there were not given an accurate account of the lead-up to her depressive illness, the drugs she had taken and the subsequent medication and ECT sessions that had been administered. As a result she suffered a heart attack on the second day and was close to death.

After a time she was sent home and was treated by self-help groups and mental health therapists. She slowly recovered. She read extensively, trying to understand what had happened to her. With this new found knowledge, she resolved to put all that had happened behind her and move on. Her three children became a part of her life once more. But her marriage broke up and, divorced, she faced the world with courage and humility. The day will surely come when she will feel able to look back and forgive, both her family and herself.

ESTRANGED

'I need space', he said
'Just give me a break
In the room of my head
Allow me to think
To get rid of the dirt
Dished up since school!'

Oh, fool! Was this really my son
Or was it drugs and drink
Wanting space for the dead;
What did he think I had done,
Had fun leaving the marriage?

Which parent brought you up?
'My mother and I grew up together' he'd say
So, for a year and a day he hid
Estranged, adrift, defiant and sad
Lost only to me – not bad.

Did I care? Oh, yes!
Did I cry? No.
Was it my fault he was hurting so?
Now his bedroom is bare
The jury is out
There is no one to hear
If I shout.

THE GIRL IN THE SPA

I was staying with my husband at a five star hotel in the middle of green belt countryside not too far out of London. He was there for a business conference and I happened to be the Chairman's wife so felt free to do as I wished. There was a five star spa attached, converted from the Palladian stables. I had just swum in the vast pool which was blood heat with a navy blue dolphin picked out in mosaic on the bottom. I had washed my hair in the shower to get rid of the smell of chlorine from the pool and was standing in a white robe in the changing room. A towel was wound round my head, and I remember looking in the mirror and thinking how the twist and pull of it made me look younger, when the door opened and a white-coated receptionist ushered someone in with the words:

"Now, have a shower and then a long swim and in half an hour I will be here to collect you to start on the treatments your husband booked for you." She then withdrew.

My gaze fell upon a young, dark woman of average height and weight and I continued with my towelling, searching for my clothes in the locker designated to me. The dressing room was not large and was lined with small lock-up cupboards. There were two basins, two hair dryers and a large wicker basket for used towels. As I reached for my clothes I was aware that the woman was standing quite still, wrapped in a pink towelling robe (not one of the white Spa issue). Her tousled hair hung forward as she held her head low and covered her face with her hands. She was sobbing. Seeing her shaking, hunched shoulders, I fastened my bra, discarded the towel and went over to her, touching her arm.

"Oh, please don't cry," I said. "Please don't. It will pass, whatever it is that is troubling you . . . truly, it will."

I could feel her pain. I stroked her back through the pink robe.

"Are you going to swim? It's lovely in the pool. There is nobody here except us."

"I don't want to be here at all, let alone swim," she said, gulping down her sobs.

After a few moments , when she had quietened, I said,

"Would you like me to swim with you? It is so soothing just to swim."

In answer she unwrapped her robe revealing a black swimsuit.

"I have come without my bag or my mobile. I am stuck here for the entire day with no money, nothing." she said.

I went back to my locker, undressed, and put on my wet bathing suit again. Then I picked up two clean towels and guided her out of the room and into the heated pool building. I carefully spread the towels on first one and then another reclining chair. She was still crying, but quietly now.

"Would you like to talk to me about it? We are alone, we are strangers and I am old enough to be your mother."

I sat down sideways on the chair and urged her to do the same. She picked up the towel and buried her face in it, then shook back her hair and looked at me with swollen, red eyes.

"Yes," I would like to talk. I can't believe he has done this to me . . . it is my birthday."

She lay back on the chair and stuck her legs out in front of her, crossing her ankles. She pulled her pink robe more tightly across her body and stared dejectedly in front of her.

"Where have you come from this morning? Do you

live far away or are you staying in the hotel like me?"
I asked.

"When I woke up this morning I felt something was wrong. He had been up earlier and had made coffee in the kitchen. I could smell toast. He is normally slow to get going. I went into the bathroom as he came up the stairs. He said through the door that he had a surprise birthday present organised for me and that I was to put on a swimsuit, have a quick cup of coffee and get into his BMW."

She put her hands over her face again, shuddered and continued:

"I realised very quickly that he wanted to get rid of me for the day. Well, he didn't want me around."

After another pause she said, "He isn't interested in me anymore. He has changed. I sometimes think he might be ill or schizophrenic or something. There must be a reason why he is behaving as he is. We have been married for nearly four years. He works a lot from home because he is an architect." She reached into her pocket for a tissue and blew her nose.

"My name is Amy. What's yours?"

"It's Susie. So did you do as he asked and get into the car?"

"Well, I flipped. It was a give-away when he told me to put on my swimming suit. I knew he had a health spa in mind. I said I didn't want to spend the day beside an indoor pool and he said nonsense, it will calm your nerves and do you good and I just lost it and screamed at him. Then he said coldly that he had spoken to the staff and arranged massages, manicures and hairdressing and would come back to collect me at 5 o'clock. He went to my chest of drawers and found this black costume and threw it at me and waited while I pulled it on. Then he got my pink robe and he gripped my arms so that I cried out with pain and he said I was hysterical. He frog-marched me downstairs and into his car. I was crying so much I could barely see . . . anyway, I was past caring. I think he told the staff here that I was a neurotic, probably having a nervous breakdown. That is what he tells his family and friends."

She turned to look at me again. I clearly read her anger, her fear of rejection, the hurtful betrayal.

"Amy," I began, reaching over to touch her arm where I could see clear evidence of recent bruising, "This too will pass . . . and remember that, in the scheme of things, the pain you are suffering will also strengthen you in the –"

She cut in, "There is someone else – I know that. There are signs. He is taking more interest in his looks, buying new clothes, washing his hair every day, refusing second helpings. I have been in deep denial. I have never brought my suspicions to the surface before. I have told no one until now. What should I do? I am so terribly angry. That is my overriding emotion. I am not much bothered by humiliation, loss of pride. Of course, there is a fear of being abandoned, but I would rather be on my own than married to someone who doesn't love me, isn't happy with me."

"No babies?" I asked.

"No babies," she replied. Tears started again. I asked her if she would like to swim but she shook her head. "But that is by choice. Deep down, I did not feel confident enough. He seemed to undermine my confidence in so many ways. Resentment grew. I have not been happy for a long time. We were not connecting . . . I feel as though I have been kidnapped. What am I doing here?"

"Shall we swim now?" I asked and rose to my feet.

Amy did not follow me down the gentle steps but walked slowly up to the far end where she dived in. She swam the considerable length of the pool under water. She emerged near me, took a breath and swam back under water again. At the deep end she surfaced, jet black hair dripping wet, and gripped the side, waiting for me to swim close.

Then she said,

"You see, he is in love with my sister. She is the 'other woman' who is probably in my own bed with my husband as I speak." Her voice rose and echoed around

211

the high ceiling as she shouted out the lines from the nursery jingle:

> 'Adam and Eve and Pinch-Me
> Went down to the sea to bathe
> Adam and Eve were drowned
> So who do you think was saved?'

"Oh, Pinch-me-not," she cried.

Turning to face me and smiling at last, she said,

"I will not let myself be so hurt again. You have helped to save me . . . from myself."

POSTON

Garden of our making, time expired
We must dress you in mourning
And bid you adieu
Drape you in purple damsons
and elderberries
Rosemary and rue –
Red for blood and white for pain
And graveyard yew
Bay for remembrance
In swatches of grief
We shall bury you deep, you two
Who knew the secret places.

ON LEAVING THE MARCHES

This is hill-billy country. Beautiful but beleaguered, polluted by the detritus left behind by the people who live there: weathered mountain folk with feuding frontier blood in their veins. Little is taken at face value and, although often heavy underfoot, they tend to be light on charm.

Herefordshire was one of the last counties in England to have panes of glass in the windows and electric light. Until quite recently there were those who seemed not to know that incest is a crime. Sheer survival has honed the spirit, but shrewd and resourceful though they are, they all too often vandalise their environment by ploughing up ancient hedgerows at night with give-away headlights on mammoth machinery. They erect barns embedded in concrete on virgin slopes which look like malignant toadstools of galvanised steel, large enough to house aircraft. Trees are used as gateposts, the gate being brutally nailed onto the trunk with heavy hinges. Discarded cars fail to die as they lie in elephant graveyards picked over by sheep and cattle.

The bread dough is delivered to the village shops deep frozen in sausages marked 'home-made granary', 'wholemeal' or 'cottage'. Potatoes are for sale at garages: 'Nadine: creamy flesh firm and moist', 'Estima: light yellow skin, light yellow flesh', 'Romano: Red skin, creamy flesh' and 'King Edward: white skin with pink patches'. The chip pan is alive and spitting every evening. Car boot sales generate a profitable swill, but the livestock sales a heart-breaking despair. The windsock on the microlight field has blown away and the river has broken its banks again and run through the caravan park. Hidden behind screens of leylandii hedges are gulags of intensively reared chickens smelling of fetid feet. County grandees, hidebound and hypocritical, are forever looking over their shoulders for lost wealth, worth and influence. Like their mediaeval cathedral, their statement has become an uncertain one, failing somehow to deliver.

There is little dignity in deprivation but there is a majesty in the natural world around me, in the land itself and in the ravens and buzzards, woodpeckers and redstarts – birds and beasts listening to life's drumbeat and hearing what we have forgotten. In the wide sky, the far horizon, the Black Mountain glacial scars and ridges, the cruel gales and the sometime silence.

I am an observer, an outsider, born in Burma, brought up in Dorset and educated in Somerset. The red earth of Herefordshire is a culture shock, but I have come to understand how it bears fruit. Its largesse is everywhere.

Waving defiantly like a small Tibetan prayer flag, anchored with two drawing pins to the weather-worn front door of the school in Much Dewchurch that my young grand-daughter, Lucy, attends, is the Steiner slogan which could well, in time, be the ultimate panacea:

'Educating From The Inside Out'

SEA OF SILK AND HONEY

These lazy waves
Replete with all the good things in life
Suck right back on themselves
And curl under before they break, white crested,
As they sneeze loudly upon the perfect beach:
The water comes home
In Royal Palm leaf shapes, fanlike,
Spewing and stirring up pieces of coral
And spreads out a Bajan sun-rug
Of finest silk beneath my feet.

Barbados, 2002.

STIRRUP CUP

Some houses have a heartbeat, a pulse of energy that is either felt or heard, like our courtyard clock above the arch in Colen Campbell's eighteenth century stable block. The horses are long since gone, but cobbles remain and a sweet smell of hot bran mash lingers in what is now the picture gallery. The clock is large and circular, hands gold leafed upon a black iron face. Lovingly restored by William Potts & Sons of Leeds, its tick is reassuringly loud and its mellow chimes are silent during the dark hours.

Some houses have a resident ghost or even a curse. ('The eldest son shall never inherit'). I have yet to hear hooves strike the cobbles, the rattle of harness or a mare's whinny. It is not difficult to be haunted by those whom you love. I dream frequently of dogs I have owned, both alive and dead. Some houses have rooms which feel uncomfortable, some have a strange smell or presence and corridors with a definite air of threat, but I do not think that house ghosts manifest themselves very often to house guests.

In my family the story goes that a house guest in the early part of the last century asked to be allowed to hunt with the Blackmore Vale. The following morning a groom was despatched to hack the best hunter to the meet at Marnhull, a village six miles away. The sky was clear and frost decorated tall grasses. The scent would be good.

Later that evening the family gathered before dinner and eagerly questioned their guest from London, wanting to know which coverts had been drawn and where they had killed. Jack, for that was his name, filled in the details but admitted to being tired as he had not arrived back until dark because his horse had nearly cast a shoe at the start of the long hack home. Luckily though, he had found himself near imposing crested iron gates to a drive and, supposing the owners of the house which must surely be at its end to be known to his friends, he opened them and rode on until he came upon a large grey stone Palladian house.

At this point in his story he was aware of an incredulous hush around him. To wide-eyed attention and gaping mouths he described how he had dismounted and pulled the bell-rope at the front door. A man had opened it to explain that his master was away. On hearing of the problem of the loose shoe he summoned a groom who secured it in a matter of minutes. In gratitude Jack gave the man a quarter sovereign, bade farewell and rode back to Fontmell Magna.

After he had finished speaking the silence was broken by his host asking for the exact location of the house described. Having heard Jack's account he told him to be ready to set out the following morning in the gig so that he could show him where he had been.

The next day, after passing through Dorset's narrow lanes, they came upon the decorated iron gates and proceeded up the long drive until they came upon the house. It stood there, an utter ruin overgrown with ivy and nettles, a sad reminder of past grandeur with a heap of rubble strewn about and large blocks of Purbeck stone. Silently the two men descended from the gig and mounted the flight of shallow steps to stand under the six remaining columns which were all that was left of the portico. As they turned to leave they saw that on the top step lay a quarter sovereign.

The idea of a Midnight Steeplechase taking place under a full moon is a bewitching one. With the building of roads and railways the race was gradually phased out although there are one or two sometimes held for the benefit of charity. The horses were ridden by jockeys dressed in white nightgowns and nightcaps. The event was held over fairly flat country, literally from church steeple to church steeple. It drew large crowds and frantic betting. As with the famous *palio* in Sienna the riders rode bareback and the value of the winning horse was greatly enhanced overnight.

I have come to realise that there are two quite different methods to adopt in order to remain in the saddle of life and not become unseated by a Beechers Brook. One is to ride short and take up your stirrup leathers a notch or two with knees pressed firmly together. Shorten the reins and hold on grimly, thumb knuckles pointing skywards. Lean well forward and exude confidence. The other technique is that you should let your leathers down several holes and ride long. Lengthen the reins with hands together held low and close to your body and be sure to lean back and let the horse have its head.

My mother's distant cousin, Jack Stratton, rode to hounds in later life when he was all but blind. He followed a white pony ridden by his boy groom over the chalk downs along the river valleys of the South & West Wilts hunt country. He rode long and into his ninetieth year.

There is a rhythm to all things. If you can hear it and rise and fall in step, then your ride through life might turn out to be a smooth one. Although some people think the stirrup cup being offered is only half full, while others believe it to be half empty, we are all competing in the same midnight steeplechase and shall arrive at the finishing post when our time comes.

DOGDAYS

These dogdays of hindsight
lie belly up
Neatly cut and stacked like turf
left to dry on the shore
No touchstone or plumb line on the
straining bladderwrack of lives
lost to the yearning for more –
And all the time, this tidal time
asking, asking
Is this all?

The Outer Hebrides

CROCHET HOOKS

The Skye Bridge is a Bridge of Sighs, cutting a swathe through Gavin Maxwell's Ring of Bright Water and Kathleen Raine's Lost Paradise.

Is not an island instantly diminished by a brutal joining to the mainland when its special identity becomes blurred at the edges? The hump-backed silver bridge from Kyle of Lochalsh over to Skye is not a thing of beauty, unlike the other brave new bridge – the majestic Severn Bridge painted in graded colours of green, grey and aquamarine. No, Skye's dumpy bridge feels as though it was an afterthought rather than a necessity, a crochet hook.

We journey on to another island, Harris in the Outer Hebrides, which is not an island at all, being joined to the considerable land mass of Lewis. Desolate, almost treeless, this is a wilderness with an undertow of powerful beauty and an air of discontent. Eagles fly and otters play and salmon gather at the river mouths to attempt a compulsive and dangerous journey to the place where they were born. Later, as we steam out of Stornoway harbour on the Ullapool ferry, the black fin of a killer whale, the size of a mainsail, slices through the millpond sea.

'There is trouble in the family', used to be knowingly said. As a family we will be found wanting this summer. One member is sleepwalking into marriage while another endures the agonies of a sick marriage. Others cannot communicate and cannot understand. My grandmother would have said how 'vexing' she found it all.

How true the words of Oscar Wilde: 'When we are young we love our parents and as we grow older we judge them, and sometimes we forgive them.' Alas, the jury is still out when their time comes, leaving uncertainty hovering like a crown of thorns until the mist clears and we can see how to bridge the gap.

Venice has more bridges to the square mile than anywhere else. The poor souls who stumbled from the Court in the Doges Palace across the canal to the foetid hell of a dungeon haunt us still. John Donne's 'No man is an island' and the Thomas Aquinas dictum 'Know Thyself!' are linked in my mind.

We are born and die alone, and it is in the interaction of living in the knitting muddles in which we find ourselves that crossings are made from our own particular island to the mainland, and many of them are inevitably over a Bridge of Sighs.

LUCY'S MUSIC

I am high on the curlew's cry,
   addicted to its call for renewal
      which moves me and draws me forward,
         staunching life's undertow.

This visiting bird of graceful beak
   and sublime song-giving
      starts soft and low –
         then rising in scale
            bursts into ecstatic crescendo

And, for me, strikes a chord of climax
   and a reason for living.

Studley Royal
April 2004